Opportunity for all
in a world of change

Presented to Parliament by the
Secretary of State for Trade and Industry and the
Secretary of State for Education and Employment
by Command of Her Majesty
February 2001

Cm 5052

£10.80

© **Crown Copyright 2001**

The text in this document may be reproduced free of charge in any format or media without requiring specific permission. This is subject to the material not being used in a derogatory manner or in a misleading context. The source of the material must be acknowledged as Crown copyright and the title of the document must be included when being reproduced as part of another publication or service.

Any enquiries relating to the copyright in this document should be addressed to HMSO, The Copyright Unit, St Clements House, 2–16 Colegate, Norwich NR3 1BQ. Fax 01603-723000 or e-mail: copyright@hmso.gov.uk

A WHITE PAPER ON ENTERPRISE, SKILLS AND INNOVATION

Contents

5 Foreword

6 Executive summary

CHAPTER 1
12 The foundations of economic success

CHAPTER 2
20 A people first economy

CHAPTER 3
34 All regions to prosper

CHAPTER 4
52 Investing in new sources of business success

CHAPTER 5
66 A climate for enterprise and growth

CHAPTER 6
74 Global ambition

84 Conclusion

A WHITE PAPER ON ENTERPRISE, SKILLS AND INNOVATION

Foreword

This White Paper sets out how the Government will work with individuals, communities and businesses to help them create opportunity through change. We offer an active, enabling Government which equips people to adapt to the rapid economic and social changes which face them, and opens up new opportunities for industries.

We inherited a boom and bust economy, poor standards in education and training, and an approach to our regions and communities which was characterised by indifference and neglect. We have put in place the framework for economic stability, raised standards in education and begun to help people build stronger communities.

Now we need to move forward, building on our achievements, to develop further the key building blocks to enable business, people and communities in all regions to take advantage of the great opportunities opened up by globalisation and technological change.

We reject the view that there is no role for Government in helping to achieve this success in a changing world.

We must ensure that people can obtain the learning and skills they need to take on new challenges at work; help the new industries and businesses of the future develop and succeed; encourage existing industries and firms to transform themselves; and widen the circle of winners so that individuals, businesses and communities in all our regions can benefit from change.

In this way, we can provide increased security within and between jobs, overcome resistance to change, and assist people through painful transitions. Through investment in key supply side measures, including re-skilling and support for enterprise and innovation, Government can enable individuals and businesses to meet the challenge of international competition.

Our vision is for a United Kingdom in which businesses, communities and individuals embrace change and seize new opportunities to prosper. That is the goal which this White Paper seeks to deliver.

The Rt Hon Stephen Byers
Secretary of State for Trade and Industry

The Rt Hon David Blunkett
Secretary of State for Education and Employment

A WHITE PAPER ON ENTERPRISE, SKILLS AND INNOVATION

Executive summary

The Goal

1 This White Paper is about the vital next steps that Government, businesses and individuals must take to secure economic success in the decade ahead. We can and must reach for this goal now. The stable economic environment that the Government has created provides a unique opportunity to reinforce strengths and remedy weaknesses that are exposed more sharply by the pressures of change.

2 To achieve improved living standards and opportunity for all we must create the conditions for everyone and every part of the nation to make the most of their talents and capabilities.

The Foundations of Economic Success

3 The Government has taken major steps to lay the foundations for businesses to grow and prosper and for individuals to succeed. We have set the framework for economic stability and sustainable growth, taking the politics out of monetary policy. That is why we now have the lowest inflation and long-term interest rates for over 30 years. We have over a million more people in work than in 1997 and the lowest ever corporation tax rate. We have reduced Government borrowing by £44 billion. For every pound of public expenditure, only 17 pence now goes to fund debt interest, unemployment benefit and social security – down from 42 pence in every pound in 1997.

4 We have acted to boost education and improve the infrastructure in telecommunications, e-commerce and transport. We have created a strong competition regime and encouraged increasing investment and research and development (R&D) through tax and other measures so that enterprise and innovation are strengthened. With these firm foundations, we now have a once in a generation opportunity to build the path towards a prosperous future.

5 The Government's analysis of the competitive challenge, set out initially in our 1998 White Paper (*Our Competitive Future: Building the Knowledge Driven Economy,* Cm 4176) has been borne out by developments over the past two years. In addition, according to the Government's November 2000 paper, *Productivity in the UK* (published by HM Treasury), UK productivity, however measured, lags behind that of other major industrialised countries. The challenge for the Government is to achieve its long-term economic ambition to have a faster rise in productivity than its main competitors and so close that gap. British businesses can no longer compete on the basis of low cost, low value added activity. To be successful, it is even more important for businesses and individuals to learn new skills, be more creative and innovative and use their knowledge to produce higher value added goods and services. Manufacturing continues to play an essential role but it too must transform itself to succeed in an increasingly global market.

6 This is a challenge that each of us can recognise in our daily lives. Whether we work for a small or large company, in manufacturing or in services, in an office or on the shop floor, all of us can see that the way we work is being transformed by new technology and new competitive pressures.

7 The coming together of these forces means that our competitiveness as a nation, our livelihoods and our quality of life increasingly depend on our ability to manage and respond to change. Our competitive advantage will only be secured through innovation and improved quality and the better use of our creativity and skills.

8 Government has a responsibility to serve as an enabling force, providing the right support for businesses and individuals to achieve success and prosperity – and in so doing widening the circle of winners in all regions and communities. Its role is to identify and anticipate the forces that are transforming the world we live in and to help people to respond to them.

9 We need an active industrial policy which recognises that change itself needs to be managed and that people need to be equipped to make the most of the new opportunities that will be created. It is not the Government's role to try to resist the profound structural changes affecting businesses and individuals, or to intervene by trying to pick winners. But equally, Government cannot stand aside and retreat from any active role in promoting security and prosperity.

10 This White Paper sets out how Government can help businesses and individuals anticipate and respond to change: working to equip individuals with the skills, abilities and know-how they need; building capacity in all communities and regions to grasp the opportunities; ensuring that investment occurs in the modern infrastructure needed to allow businesses and individuals to innovate and compete; increasing the possibilities for people to transform their ideas into successful businesses and ensuring markets operate effectively and fairly in the best interests of consumers; strengthening the European and global frameworks to maximise opportunity and wealth creation.

A People First Economy

11 The Government inherited a situation of poor standards in schools, millions of adults lacking in the basic skills of literacy and numeracy and an undervalued system of vocational and technical education.

12 We have already made substantial progress in tackling these problems. Primary schools are delivering the best ever results in literacy and numeracy. The basis has been laid for the high quality expansion of university places. More than 600,000 adults have opened Individual Learning Accounts. We must now press ahead to ensure that our people learn to be creative and enterprising and that they have the world beating technical skills they need, through training and education at all levels.

13 We will:
- foster creativity and enterprise across our education and training system through radical new approaches to teaching and learning and through much more extensive links between education and business;
- ensure we have a numerate and literate population, reducing the number of adults with literacy and numeracy problems by 750,000 by 2004 and spending an extra £150 million on literacy and numeracy training;
- build a world class vocational and technical education system through a major rationalisation of vocational qualifications up to technician level by Autumn 2001, investing £100 million to develop vocational specialisms in colleges and more resources in reformed Modern Apprenticeships;
- develop a workforce with world beating information and communication technology (ICT) skills by training up to 10,000 more people a year through new advanced learning programmes and widening the pool of recruitment into ICT including moving 5,000 unemployed people into ICT jobs over the next three years; and
- ensure that employers invest in the skills and talents of all by setting clear and auditable targets for training, investing £45 million in a smaller, stronger network of National Training Organisations and helping small firms to collaborate on training.

All Regions to Prosper

14 Our aim is to increase the trend rate of growth in all regions by addressing under-performance, building on success and promoting enterprise for all. We need a new approach to regional policy to enable people and businesses to respond to change. We must strengthen the building blocks for economic success which are the key to innovation in a knowledge economy.

15 The Government will:
- establish top class university innovation centres and new technology institutes in the regions to boost research and development, innovation and technology transfer and to provide the regions with skills in ICT and high technology;
- boost the capacity for enterprise in all regions by launching a new £75 million incubator fund, managed by the Small Business Service, to support new business formation; ensuring support is available at the right time for growth businesses; and developing new funding to fill gaps in the availability of small amounts of risk capital for new and growing businesses, including those which rely on intangible assets;
- give special support to manufacturing industry by establishing a new Manufacturing Advisory Service;
- promote the growth of successful clusters, building on existing strengths and with the assistance of the clusters map published by DTI. Regional Development Agencies are already taking steps to identify and encourage emerging clusters, for example chemicals, electronics and automotive in the North East;
- remove constraints to growth by inviting the Regional Development Agencies to develop strategies for success in their regions;
- implement the new Job Transition Service, managed by the Employment Service, to enable individuals affected by large-scale redundancy to find the right jobs more quickly and help growing companies tackle skill shortages; and
- make the planning system quicker and more efficient, boosting the regional skills base and improving regional and local transport infrastructure.

Investing in New Sources of Business Success

16 The Government has invested heavily in the UK's university research, infrastructure and skills base. But we need to do more to keep ahead and spread the benefits of new research to business. By taking up and adapting new technologies we can develop new world beating industries and transform established sectors.

17 The Government will:
- provide £90 million, to complement recent investment under the science budget, to promote the commercial exploitation of research focusing on genomics, basic technologies and e-science;
- encourage development and take-up of more resource efficient and environmentally friendly products and energy systems, by promoting markets for new technologies which reduce waste and by embarking on a major initiative with industry and others to achieve a UK solar photovoltaic demonstration programme in line with those of our main competitors;
- accelerate the take-up of broadband technology by businesses and households. Our aim is for the UK to have the most extensive and competitive broadband market in the group of seven leading industrialised nations by 2005 and as a first step we are providing £30 million for innovative schemes to meet local requirements;
- boost digital TV which will transform the communications services available in the home and open up new markets and service opportunities. Our aim is for the UK to have the most dynamic and competitive market for digital TV in the group of seven leading industrialised nations, as measured by take-up, choice and cost;
- stimulate the development of content for the digital technologies; and
- provide a further £30 million to increase awareness and understanding among all businesses of the challenges and opportunities of e-business and new ways of working in transformed organisations.

A Climate for Enterprise and Growth

18 To succeed in the global economy of the twenty-first century, the UK must have a regulatory and financial environment which is second to none in fostering enterprise and growth. The Government will:
- significantly relax insolvency rules so that honest businesses and individuals who go bankrupt have a better chance of starting again quicker, while cracking down on the fraudulent or irresponsible;
- adopt a more commercial approach to company rescue proposals put to them by companies in short-term financial difficulty;
- give the Office of Fair Trading a new pro-competitive role to spot existing and proposed regulations which hold back dynamic and competitive markets;
- drive forward the Small Business Service strategy "Think Small First" which requires Government Departments to consider the implications for small businesses when developing policy or proposing regulations; and
- the Small Business Service will launch, by the Summer, a set of initiatives to help small businesses better understand external investment and become better prepared to take it on.

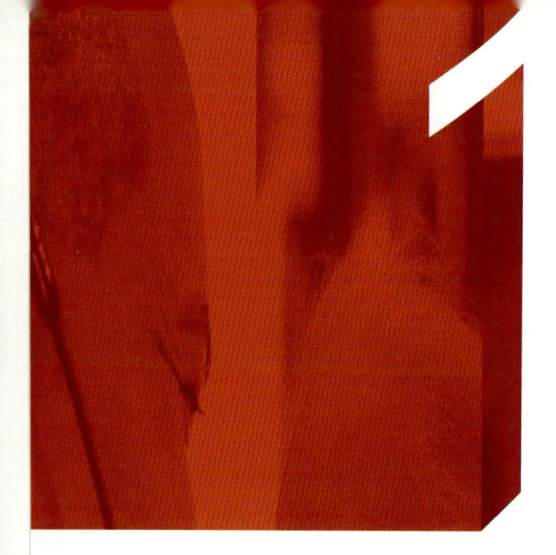

A WHITE PAPER ON ENTERPRISE, SKILLS AND INNOVATION

The foundations of economic success

Introduction

1.1 This White Paper is about the vital next steps that Government, businesses and individuals must take now to secure sustainable economic success in the decade ahead. Our success in this will affect more than business alone. It will determine how individuals achieve a better quality of life and how communities and regions grow and prosper. We can only extend opportunity, invest in public services, deliver decent pensions and pay for a first class education and health system if we meet this challenge.

The Role of Government

1.2 Each of us makes our living in an economic environment which is changing rapidly and fundamentally. Our competitiveness as a nation and our livelihoods as individuals increasingly depend on our ability to manage and respond to this change, securing our competitive advantage through our skills, innovation and creativity.

1.3 Businesses and individuals play the central role in this. But we are firmly of the view that Government has a vital proactive part to play. Government has a responsibility to serve as an enabling force, providing the right support to achieve success and prosperity — and in so doing widening the circle of winners in all regions and communities.

1.4 Government can do this by identifying and anticipating the forces that are transforming the world we live in and helping people to respond to them. It must involve and prepare people and communities, at home and at work, so that they can be partners in change and not its innocent victims. We need an active industrial policy which recognises that change itself needs to be managed and that people need to be equipped to make the most of the new opportunities that will be created.

1.5 We cannot and should not try to resist the profound structural changes affecting businesses and individuals. Industrial policy today is not about picking winners, propping up losers or running businesses from Whitehall.

1.6 But equally we reject the idea that Government should just stand aside and retreat from any active role in promoting security and prosperity – surrendering to the worst consequences of global, social and economic changes rather than trying to shape them in ways that are good for our people. The pressures of globalisation and intensified competition are not abstract forces but have a direct effect on people as they go about their lives and on the communities in which they live.

1.7 The Government has already taken major steps to lay the foundations of economic success. We have set the framework for macroeconomic stability and taken the politics out of monetary policy. That is why we now have the lowest inflation and long term interest rates for over 30 years. We have the lowest ever corporation tax rate. Over 1.1 million more people are now in work than in 1997 and Government borrowing has been cut by £44 billion. As a consequence, for every pound of public expenditure only 17 pence now goes to fund debt interest, unemployment benefit and social security – down from 42 pence in every pound in 1997. We have acted to boost education and improve the infrastructure in telecommunications and transport. We have created a strong competition regime and encouraged increasing investment and research and development (R&D) through tax and other measures to spur enterprise and innovation.

Our Goal

1.8 Our goal is to improve living standards and opportunity for all. This means creating the conditions for everyone and every part of the UK to make the most of their talents and capabilities.

1.9 We can and must reach for this goal now. The stable economic environment that we have created provides a unique opportunity to reinforce strengths and remedy weaknesses that are exposed more sharply by the pressures of change.

The Challenge of Change

1.10 The powerful currents that are reshaping our economic lives are the product of a combination of factors. Some – the rise of the service sector, the growth of international trade and investment, the liberalisation of financial markets – have taken many decades to develop. Others – the spread of the Internet, mobile telephones, our growing understanding of the human genome – have emerged only in the past few years. The consequences of these changes will be as significant both economically and socially as the changes we witnessed in the nineteenth century when we moved from an agriculturally based economy to an industrial one.

1.11 Economies are constantly subject to change. Sectors of the economy expand and contract over time and resources move between them, generally into higher value added activities. The most obvious recent change has been the growth in the size of the service sector, caused partly by the outsourcing of operations previously carried out within manufacturing companies, and partly by increased demand for services as income rises. This change in the relative share of manufacturing in the UK has been mirrored in all advanced economies. Nevertheless the absolute level of UK manufacturing output has continued to rise. Within manufacturing, the share of some sectors has grown significantly (for example, aerospace, motor vehicles, computers, office machinery and communications equipment) while the share of others has declined (for example basic metals, textiles and food).

1.12 The pace and significance of change can also be seen in the changing composition of the FT Stock Exchange 100. Over a half of the companies in the current top 100 are new entrants since 1984, many of them from the information technology, utilities and business service sectors, replacing firms in basic industries. These shifts are reflected in changes in the labour market. Job gains in the service sector have significantly outweighed job losses in manufacturing and the total number of people in work hit an all-time high in 2000.

The foundations of economic success

1.13 Manufacturing continues to play an integral role in any growing and prosperous economy. As living standards rise, consumers continue to want manufactured goods. Globalisation is widening the range of suppliers from whom they can buy as is the case with every sector where, thanks to the Internet, the competition is just a click away. For manufacturers in the advanced economies the challenge is to be at the leading edge, offering consumers more innovative products made to a higher quality and more efficiently. Some of the most successful manufacturers are redesigning their businesses around providing their customers with a stream of services.

1.14 The Government's analysis of the competitive challenge we face, set out initially in our 1998 White Paper (*Our Competitive Future: Building the Knowledge Driven Economy,* Cm 4176) has been borne out by developments over the past two years. In addition, according to the Government's November 2000 paper, *Productivity in the UK* (published by HM Treasury), UK productivity, however measured, lags behind that of other major industrialised countries. The challenge for Government is to achieve its long-term economic ambition to have a faster rise in productivity than its main competitors and so close that gap. To be successful, it is even more important for businesses and individuals to learn new skills and to use their knowledge to produce higher value added goods and services.

1.15 This is a challenge each of us can recognise in our daily lives. Whether we work for a small or large company, in manufacturing or in services, in an office or on the shop floor, all of us can see that the way we work is being transformed by new technology and new competitive pressures.

1.16 Over the next decade, many of the general features of the economic changes we can expect are clear:
- the world economy is likely to become even more integrated through trade, investment and communications;
- investment in science and innovation will create ever more products and services and entirely new industries;
- consumers will demand not just low prices but high quality, good design, effective customer service and products that combine several technologies;
- there will be increasing demand for those who are adaptable and have high occupational and technical skills and less demand for people with low skills;
- manufacturing will remain an important part of the economy but the line between manufacturing, technology and services will increasingly blur as successful manufacturers adopt new ways of working and organise production among networks of companies;
- communications and the spread of knowledge around the world will continue to accelerate through increased investment in education, not least in the developing world, and through steep falls in the cost of computing and communications and the creation of broadband infrastructures;
- the Internet will become an essential tool for businesses in their trade with each other and their customers but it will not in itself guarantee success unless it is combined with sound business basics, most obviously a good product and effective logistics;
- there will be more innovation in the creative and content industries as the impact of the knowledge economy grows; and
- global pressures on resources and the environment will accelerate the trend towards greener technologies. The demands of improving resource productivity require far reaching changes to the way we design, manufacture, market, use and dispose of products.

Where the UK Stands

1.17 The UK is in some ways well placed to meet the challenges of a globally integrated, innovation-driven economy. In other respects, it is less prepared. We are publishing the *UK Competitiveness Indicators: Second Edition*, a comprehensive analysis with more than 40 indicators of the UK's strengths and weaknesses compared with its major international competitors.

1.18 We have a strong position in the knowledge-based sector which includes fast-growing manufacturing and service industries such as telecommunications, fibre optics, biotechnology, pharmaceuticals, aerospace and the creative industries. Our science base is respected around the world and our universities are at the leading edge of innovation and knowledge creation. These areas must not be neglected and we need to consolidate our position.

How We Will Meet the Challenge

1.19 This White Paper outlines the practical policies and programmes through which Government can carry out its role. It shows:

- how we can work to equip individuals with the skills, abilities and know-how they need to be successful in the modern economy;
- how we can ensure that the communities and the regions within which people live have the capacity to grasp the opportunities offered by change, particularly through expanding research and development, knowledge creation and upgrading skills;
- how we can ensure that investment occurs in the modern infrastructure needed to allow businesses and individuals to innovate, compete and contribute to a sustainable future;
- how we can increase the possibilities for everyone to take forward their ideas into successful business and ensure that markets operate effectively and fairly in the best interests of consumers; and
- how we can make sure the European and global framework is one which maximises opportunity and wealth creation.

Improving Technical and Basic Skills and Enhancing Creativity and Enterprise

1.20 The emerging economy puts a premium on skills and knowledge at all levels but particularly on creativity and the ability to innovate, information and communication technologies (ICT) skills, other technical skills as well as the basic ability to read and write. We are publishing today the Government's detailed response to the final report of the National Skills Task Force which covers these and related issues.

1.21 We have already made substantial progress in meeting the need for these skills. Our primary and secondary school pupils are achieving the best ever results in literacy and numeracy and in GCSEs. All have the opportunity to pursue broader programmes of study post-16 that encourage creativity, innovation and the development of communication, number and ICT skills. Record numbers go on to higher education and our graduation rate is amongst the highest in the world.

1.22 Yet while there has been a radical improvement in educational attainment, too many 16 year olds left school in 2000 with low or no GCSEs. Around 7 million adults in England are functionally illiterate – meaning that they read less well than the average 11 year old – according to the 1999 report of Sir Claus Moser's Working Group *(Improving Literacy and Numeracy for Adults: A Fresh Start)*. More than half the workforce have only low qualifications and many millions have none at all *(Labour Force Survey 1999)*. This lack of basic skills and qualifications among so many in the workforce constrains our ability to achieve full employment and to raise productivity and innovation in businesses.

The foundations of economic success

1.23 We have a shortage of technicians and ICT professionals. Although we compare well with other countries on some measures of training in the workplace, this is concentrated among a relatively small group of well educated employees. Many businesses recognise that current levels of training are insufficient to meet changing skill needs.

1.24 The Government will ensure that creativity, enterprise and the ability to innovate are at the heart of the education and skills we provide to our young people and adults. We will put in place a strategy to reduce by 750,000 the number of adults with poor reading and numeracy skills. We will reform technical and vocational training across the board to match world class standards. And we will boost the supply of ICT and high technology skills and encourage business, particularly small firms, to improve workforce training.

A New Approach to Regional Policy

1.25 Our economic performance is uneven across the country. There are marked disparities between and within UK regions. Table 1 below shows that since 1990, regional disparities have increased. GDP (gross domestic product) per head has grown significantly faster in the South East and Northern Ireland than the average for the UK; but significantly more slowly in the North East, North West and Wales. To some extent these figures reflect the industrial composition of regions, in particular the larger contribution of manufacturing in some regions.

1.26 Ensuring that all parts and all people of the UK achieve their full potential is an economic as well as a social imperative. The Government has already allocated £1.2 billion for 2000/01 to Regional Development Agencies and this allocation will rise to £1.4 billion for 2001/02 with increased flexibilty for the Agencies to use their budgets for

TABLE 1

Regional GDP per head of population. Government Office Regions, 1990 and 1998.
GDP at basic prices, workplace basis, UK = 100

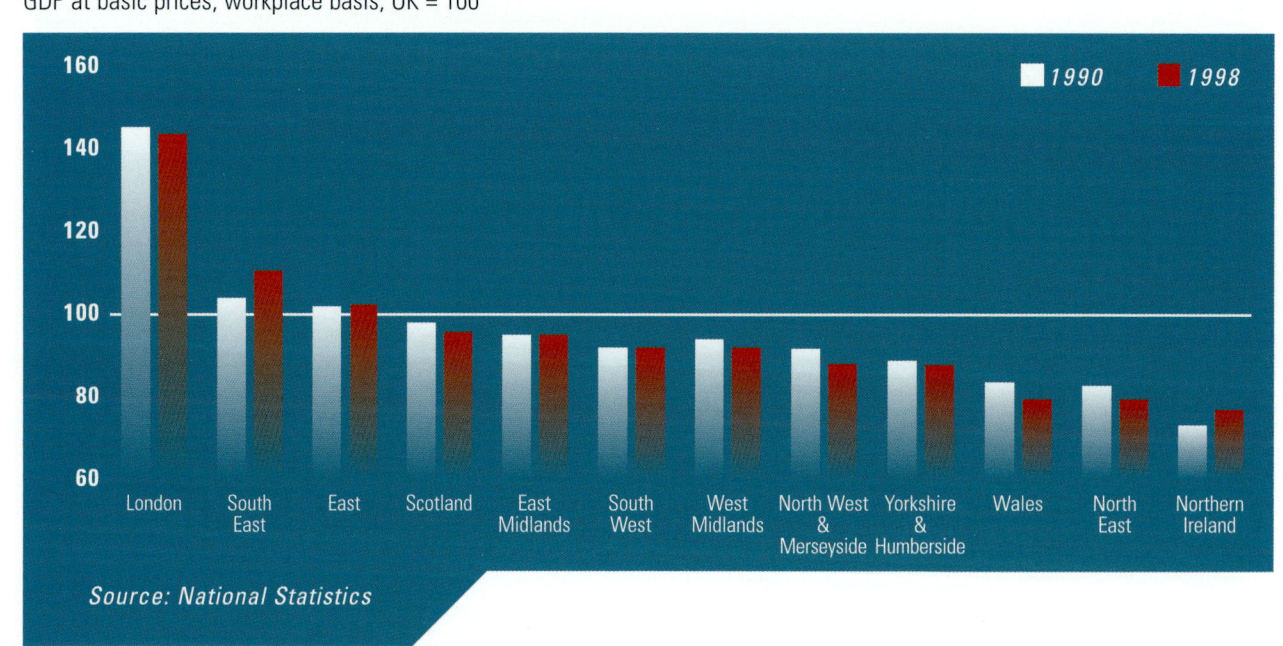

Source: National Statistics

regional priorities. This White Paper sets out a new approach to regional policy with the aim of generating hubs of growth through more start-up companies and clusters of expertise and innovation. Having a strong regional policy is essential to help localities succeed and to expand the winners' circle. We are also publishing a clusters map which can be used to assist this approach and identify where future successful clusters could emerge.

1.27 The Government will therefore strengthen the building blocks for regional economic growth: encouraging more business formation and growth; boosting research and development by pulling together the best regional brains and expertise; removing barriers to expansion of successful clusters; encouraging business flexibility and workforce skills for manufacturing businesses; helping individuals and communities respond effectively to change and restructuring.

Investing to Feed the Sources of Innovation

1.28 Economic growth and increased productivity are driven by innovation. Weaknesses in research and development can handicap innovation. On average, businesses in the group of seven leading industrialised nations except Italy invest more in R&D per worker than British businesses (Table 2)

1.29 In e-commerce the picture is encouraging in some areas, but less so in others. According to a report by Merrill Lynch, the value of business to business sales in the UK is higher as a percentage of output than in any of our competitors in the group of seven leading industrialised nations except the USA. Yet although 27 per cent of UK businesses (weighted by employment) now trade online, ahead of others in the group of seven leading industrialised nations, very few businesses are fully integrating these new ways of working throughout their operations.

TABLE 2
Industry-funded business enterprise R&D (BERD) real expenditure per worker.
G7 comparison, 1988-1998.
US dollars, at 1990 prices and purchasing power parities

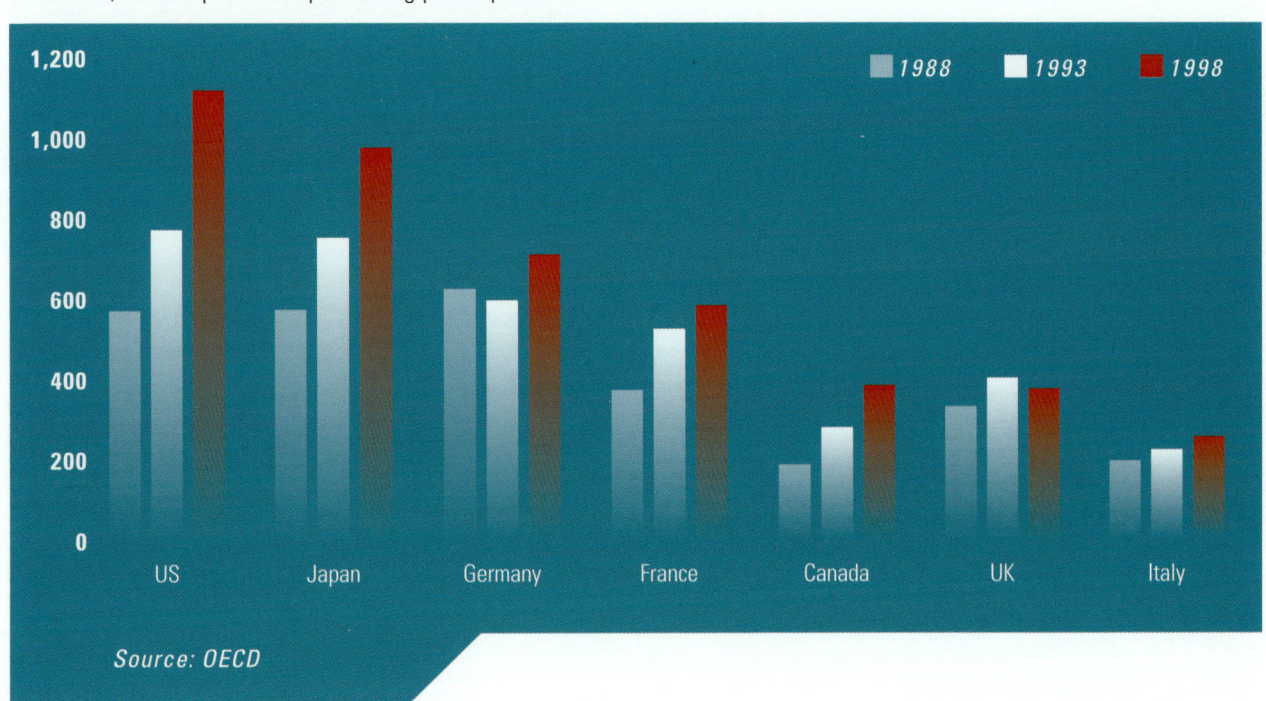

Source: OECD

1.30 The convergence between communications and computing has the potential to transform business processes and offer new opportunities to everyone. Government can accelerate the process of innovation by increasing the rate at which new knowledge and technologies can be shared and exploited.

1.31 The Government will therefore boost the emerging sources of innovation by accelerating the roll-out of the next generation of communications infrastructure – particularly broadband networks and digital TV – and by exploiting recent scientific advances in areas such as our increasing understanding of the genome, e-science and environmental technologies. We are publishing *UK online: the broadband future* which outlines the steps we will take to ensure a competitive and dynamic market for broadband services.

A Regulatory and Financial Framework for Enterprise

1.32 The UK compares well on some of the conditions for entrepreneurship. But according to the *Global Entrepreneurship Monitor* report 2000, we also lag behind our competitors in significant respects. In particular, the level of new business start-ups is significantly behind countries such as the USA and Italy, and our entrepreneurial culture is not well developed.

1.33 The UK was perceived by business in 1999/2000 to have one of the most pro-competitive economies among the group of seven leading industrialised nations, according to an Institute of Management Development survey. But in a fast moving environment, where many other nations are jostling for success, we must continue to work hard to maintain this relative advantage.

1.34 The UK's regulatory and financial framework must be second to none in encouraging rather than discouraging enterprise. The Government will therefore build on the steps we have already taken and deliver new policies to remove barriers to enterprise, prevent unnecessarily heavy-handed regulation from stifling new ideas and encourage investment. For example, the Small Business Service strategy, "Think Small First", asks all Government Departments to think about the implications for small businesses when developing policy and to consult the Small Business Service at an early stage when regulations are being considered for the UK.

Global Ambition

1.35 The UK cannot stand alone in today's globalised economy. We are part of that global environment and closely bound up with the European Union as our main market for goods and services. This fact must form a key element in our industrial policy.

1.36 We must move forward by strengthening the UK's engagement with Europe and the wider world. We must build links between people, partnerships between businesses and harness the potential of all our regions to compete in world markets by strengthening their global connections. We must continue to use our influence on the international environment to enable us to realise this vision.

1.37 There are limits to what national governments can realistically achieve on their own. In a global economy we benefit from investment by multinational companies which can go anywhere in the world. We cannot force companies to invest or to continue to invest in particular places. But we expect their decisions to be responsible ones. Government can help people adapt to change and it can influence the wider international framework in which company decisions are made.

1.38 The Government will therefore work to strengthen the UK's global links and promote the best environment in Europe and worldwide for British success, by attracting the brightest and best potential and experienced entrepreneurs to this country; strengthening support for business on the global stage; and working to improve the framework for closer global integration and to keep European economic reform on track.

Moving Forward in Harmony

1.39 All parts of the UK need to move forward in harmony, building on their own distinctive strengths. In Scotland, Wales and Northern Ireland specific initiatives and delivery mechanisms may vary from those described in this and other chapters where they apply primarily to England. Each part of the UK must find its own winning formula and will do so with assistance and encouragement from Government; but each can also share in and learn from best practice in other parts.

The foundations of economic success

A WHITE PAPER ON ENTERPRISE, SKILLS AND INNOVATION

A *people first economy*

Introduction

2.1 The success of individuals and businesses in a knowledge driven economy will depend upon the skills, creativity and imagination of our people. Basic literacy and numeracy and specialist craft and technical skills remain vital, but today's economy increasingly demands people with high level skills and the ability to adapt quickly to changing requirements. Lifelong learning and continuous reskilling are essential to enable people to cope with change, achieve security in their lives and benefit from growing prosperity.

2.2 We are at an historic point in the development of our education and training system. The reforms we are engaged in will allow us to leave behind the failures of more than a century and look forward to a modern skills system attuned to the demands of the twenty-first century. For business they offer the prospect of increased skill levels in the workforce. For individuals they offer the prospect of a route to skills that are valued in the labour market and that will help maintain them in stable and well-rewarded employment. Our aim is a transformation to create a highly skilled workforce, and highly productive businesses and organisations across the country – working at the leading edge of technology. We must have opportunities for all, unleash creativity and talent, and seize the opportunities of the next decade.

Where the UK Stands

2.3 The Government inherited a situation in which four out of ten of our children left primary schools unable to read, write and count properly, and far too few young people achieved good GCSE passes. It inherited a situation in which millions of adults lacked the basic skills of literacy and numeracy, and in which too few were involved in learning. And it inherited a weak, undervalued system of vocational and technical education.

2.4 We have taken responsibility for tackling these fundamental problems because we believe that Government has a crucial role in helping people develop the skills needed for economic prosperity and social cohesion. Already substantial progress has been made:

- our young people are better educated and qualified than ever before as a result of higher standards of teaching and learning. Primary schools have delivered the best ever results in literacy and numeracy, and more young people achieve five or more higher grades at GCSE;
- young people are gaining the knowledge, skills and flexibility required for work and lifelong learning through new vocational courses, broader A-level studies, and the achievement of key skills in communication, number and information technology;
- standards have been raised in further education, and we have injected the biggest ever investment of extra funding into the sector – £759 million over the next two years, which is 16 per cent in real terms;
- tough decisions on student funding have secured the resources necessary for sustainable, high quality expansion of university places. Record numbers enter higher education, and Britain's graduation rate is now among the highest in the world. Our universities are at the leading edge of knowledge creation and innovation;
- more than 600,000 people have opened new Individual Learning Accounts, which allow them to benefit from a wide range of learning at discounted rates, giving people the chance to take control of how they manage and pay for their learning, helping to boost their employability, their earning power and their quality of life. And **learndirect**, the customer brand for the Ufi, has begun to provide cost effective and accessible online learning to business and individuals.

The Unipart Group has introduced an online learning system, 'Virtual U', designed to deliver electronic courses to the company's 10,000 employees. **learndirect** products and services will be available to staff through the 'Virtual U' which will deliver web-based courses direct to the employee's desktop PC. Unipart will also become a Ufi hub, administering the provision of **learndirect** services for other companies within the automotive sector. Unipart's Group Chief Executive John Neill said, "The introduction of online learning will now enable our employees to learn at the speed of light and give them access to the knowledge and the tools they require, immediately they require it".

2.5 We have also created the Learning and Skills Council, an historic reform that will – for the first time – integrate the planning and funding of all post-16 academic and vocational learning outside higher education, enabling us to raise standards universally, and cut red tape in the delivery of skills development to businesses. The key objectives of the Learning and Skills Council will be to raise the skills of the workforce by ensuring that up to date and relevant courses are available for the continuous updating of skills, and to draw into learning those on the margins of the labour force, or who have lost their jobs as the result of industrial and economic change.

2.6 These radical initiatives form a major programme of modernisation to achieve world class education and learning for the twenty-first century and to replace outdated structures geared to the last industrial era. They are essential to implement the education and training strategy set out in our policy papers on *The Learning Age* and *Learning to Succeed*.

2.7 While good progress has been made in addressing the legacy the Government inherited, many challenges remain. There are still too many young people leaving school with no or only very low grade GCSEs and too many lack the skills to make the most of their capacity for innovation and creativity. It is unacceptable that seven million adults have difficulties with basic literacy and numeracy. We have a shortage of technicians and information and communication technology (ICT) professionals. While we compare well with other countries on some measures of training in the workplace, it is concentrated among a relatively small group of well educated employees. And we are still not making the best use of the talents of all our people – only 67 per cent of ethnic minority adults are economically active compared to 80 per cent of white adults.

2.8 In our Green Paper, *Schools – Building on Success,* we set out the further action we will take to raise standards in education. In this White Paper we set out our strategy for driving up the skills of the workforce, building on the recommendations of the National Skills Task Force.

What the Government will do

2.9 We must now build on our success and the reforms we have already put in place. We must ensure that people learn how to be creative and enterprising to generate the ideas, products and services of the future; we must raise the skills base of the adult workforce; and we must develop the cadre of people with leading edge technical skills which we have lacked for so long. Our priorities therefore are to:

- foster greater creativity, innovative thinking and enterprise across our education and training system, encourage better links between education and business, and ensure high quality teaching and learning at all levels;
- ensure that we have a numerate and literate population and engage more adults in learning to provide a stronger skills base in the workforce;
- build a vocational and technical education system which matches the best in the world;
- develop a workforce with advanced ICT skills and know-how to match the best of our competitors; and
- ensure that all employers invest in the skills and talents of all their employees.

2.10 Our approach reflects a deep commitment to ensuring that all our people have the skills they need for success. It is no longer acceptable to educate a few to think and the many to do. Government's role is to provide the framework in which individuals and employers can invest in skills and ensure equality of opportunity. Investment in skills must be shared between individuals, employers and Government. For Government, ensuring that everybody has good skills is the best way to secure equality of opportunity, social cohesion and national prosperity.

Fostering Creativity and Enterprise

2.11 People who generate bright ideas and have the practical abilities to turn them into successful products and services are vital not just to the creative industries but to every sector of business. Our whole approach to what and how we learn from the earliest stages of learning needs to adapt and change to respond to this need. Academic achievement remains essential, but it must increasingly be delivered through a rounded education which fosters creativity, enterprise and innovation. This will only be secured if teaching and learning are of a consistently high standard.

We will put in place a co-ordinated strategy for ensuring that in every sector of learning students have the opportunity, and are encouraged, to develop their creativity, capacity for innovation and understanding of enterprise. This will bring together work to reform teaching and learning, the promotion of improved links between business and education and initiatives to encourage enterprise.

2.12 Our strategy for the transformation of secondary education, particularly in the early years, will ensure the development of children's abilities to reason and to think critically, as well as improving their competence and skills in English, maths, science and ICT. Motivation, teamwork and creativity will be developed not just through the content of the curriculum but through the opportunities provided for pupils to learn about and contribute to the life and organisation of their school.

2.13 We will press ahead with introducing modern processes into schools so that young people learn to work with Computer Aided Design and Manufacture software and with electronic and communication systems. This will be part of a wider effort to teach young people the skills they will need to work effectively in project teams developing complex products in a creative environment.

2.14 Links between the worlds of education and business will continue to be fostered and developed, with added momentum from the work of the Learning and Skills Council. In addition to the fundamental reform of vocational and technical education, outlined below, including the development of vocational specialisms across further education colleges, the Learning and Skills Council will take a more co-ordinated and strategic approach to a wide range of links between education and business. With Regional Development Agencies, the Small Business Service and others, it will work to ensure that all young people have the opportunity to develop entrepreneurial ability, skills and creativity.

2.15 We will work with business to support and extend programmes which develop enterprise skills in young people. With Enterprise Insight, the private sector-led national campaign for enterprise, we will work to increase the number of businesses and entrepreneurs supporting existing education business link programmes. We will also support innovative new activities designed to develop enterprise amongst young people. New Entrepreneur Scholarships give potential entrepreneurs of all ages from deprived areas access to high quality management and business training, assisting them at all stages of the development of a business idea into reality.

2.16 In higher education, we will enhance the centres of excellence in enterprise established through Science Enterprise Challenge, and continue our strategy of driving up awareness of enterprise and business. Many universities already offer courses in entrepreneurship or offer entrepreneurial skills through other programmes of study, and we will promote further expansion of these opportunities. We also intend to ensure a significant expansion of work experience opportunities for students, and develop far better careers advice facilities in our universities and colleges.

2.17 An education that provides creativity, enterprise and innovation to the benefit of learners and businesses depends on the very highest standards of teaching and learning, and on the ability of teachers and lecturers to enhance the way that young people learn so as to develop those capabilities. Our radical programme to raise standards in the teaching profession will be crucial:

- an ambitious reform programme is already in place to strengthen school leadership; give better pay and career prospects; and make initial teacher training better focused and more flexible, including an expansion of the Graduate Teacher Programme;
- a range of programmes is giving teachers better support, including a huge capital investment in the school environment and in ICT hardware, software and training. Twenty thousand additional classroom assistants are being trained to work in schools; and
- further reforms will strengthen the skills of serving teachers. This will include the skills needed to help young people develop strong communication abilities and benefit from individualised learning.

2.18 The Learning and Skills Council will take forward a programme of work to develop practitioner skills and qualifications in the further education sector, work-based learning, adult and community learning, and the skills for supporting and tutoring online learning. The Council will also monitor the delivery of teaching and training qualifications and continuous professional development across the post-16 sector outside higher education.

Improving Numeracy and Literacy and Engaging More Adults in Learning

2.19 In the past, too many people left school lacking basic skills. This makes it harder for them to get secure and rewarding jobs, and to play a full part in the lives of their families and communities. By failing to provide businesses with the skills they need, it also impacts severely on the productivity of the economy. The Government will launch a national basic skills strategy to tackle this silent scandal. Our national goal is to expand the horizons and capabilities of the millions of adults who have chronically weak literacy and numeracy skills and to engage more low qualified adults in learning.

The Learning and Skills Council will plan provision locally and nationally to achieve new and ambitious targets. We aim to reduce the number of adults with literacy and numeracy problems by 750,000 by 2004. Spending on literacy and numeracy training will increase by at least £150 million by 2003-04, an increase of over 60 per cent. The Learning and Skills Council will work closely with National Training Organisations and Regional Development Agencies to improve basic skills levels in key sectors of the economy, including in construction, retail, transport, road haulage and catering.

2.20 The strategy for achieving these targets will be driven forward by the Government's new Adult Basic Skills Strategy Unit in the DfEE. Working with the Basic Skills Agency and others, it will put in place a new core literacy and numeracy curriculum for adults, new National Tests, better training for teachers and robust inspection arrangements. It will establish pathfinder projects in every region to ensure that these changes lead to the improvements in standards and achievement that we expect.

2.21 Engaging adults with literacy and numeracy difficulties will require new and flexible approaches. Some of the key initiatives we will take forward are as follows:

- **learndirect** will ensure that employers can access basic skills education at a time and a place to suit their business needs. It will provide flexible and accessible basic skills education in the home, in the workplace and through a nationwide network of learning centres. Its target is to provide basic skills education to 100,000 people with 200,000 enrolments by 2003;
- we will expand funding through the Union Learning Fund specifically to support the development of literacy and numeracy skills, building on the success of work already being undertaken by all the major unions to encourage those with basic skills needs to begin training;
- we will begin action to help employers in one of our basic skills pathfinder areas where we will be piloting the use of replacement funding for employers to cover the cost of releasing employees with basic skills needs for one day a week over 13 weeks. Details of the pathfinder areas will be announced as part of the Government's basic skills strategy.

2.22 As well as helping people to fit learning alongside job and family, Government will help with the costs of learning. On top of the entitlement to free basic skills training, the Government already covers 75 per cent of further education course fees (rising to 100 per cent for unemployed people). Individual Learning Accounts also offer people further help to cover costs and give a sense of ownership of learning.

2.23 However, the Government recognises that more needs to be done to support adults who want to study further education courses. The present financial support arrangements for adult learners outside higher education are incomplete and incoherent. We plan to provide adult students with a comprehensive system of financial support which meets their varying needs. We intend to bring forward new approaches which will increase the number of funding options for these students and deliver a fairer system of student support which is responsive, simple to understand and accessible.

> Like many thousands of people, Tommy Dawkins has difficulty reading and writing. However, unlike many, he has declared these difficulties and is tackling them; and he is also encouraging his colleagues to do the same. As a learning representative at Steelite International plc, Tommy ensures that colleagues are aware of the learning opportunities open to them via their union and through the workplace. As Tommy explains, "I decided I was going to get this over to the workforce and the company as well, because you need them to be involved too. My plans for the future are to go on more courses, and carry on until I can read, write and spell with confidence." He became involved at Steelite in the Pathway to Lifelong Learning programme (a Union Learning Fund supported project), which earned the Ceramic and Allied Trade Union a Learning in the Workplace Award in recognition of its work in helping its members to return to learning.

A Vocational Education System which Matches the Best in the World

2.24 Britain needs to develop its vocational and technical education system in a way which provides young people with a high prestige alternative to exclusively academic study and ensures that employers can recruit people with the skills and knowledge they need at all levels of business activity. Throughout the twentieth century, the opportunities for vocational learning have been seen as lower level than those in academic learning, and as a consequence, the worlds of education and work were kept too far apart. Today, too many bright young people drop out of learning because academic education is neither interesting nor relevant enough to them, and large numbers enter the labour market without the skills employers need. Our objective is to create a modern, high standard system of vocational and technical education, which will meet the needs of the new century.

We will extend opportunities for 14-16 year olds to undertake vocational courses and rationalise the confusing system of vocational qualifications. We will also boost the capacity of further education to deliver high quality vocational learning and invest in improved Modern Apprenticeships.

A people first economy

2.25 Our reform of the vocational qualifications system will create a ladder of vocational opportunity for young people, with high standards throughout and result in qualifications which are clearer and better understood by employers, young people and parents alike. The key elements in the reform are that:

- we will strengthen and clarify the vocational pathways available from age 14 and in particular we will consult on the scope for increasing the time available for vocational study within the statutory framework. Our intention is that vocational options should be available to students across the ability range;
- young people who want a future career based on vocational and technical skills should be able to choose predominantly vocational programmes of study from age 14, involving practical activity in the workplace and vocational study, perhaps at a nearby college. These programmes will help young people who want to gain occupational skills through Foundation and Advanced Modern Apprenticeships after leaving school;
- just as we have broadened academic A-level study, so we will ensure that young people on vocational programmes secure broad knowledge and understanding, alongside specialist expertise and skills. The Qualifications and Curriculum Authority (QCA) will advise by the end of 2001 on the combinations of vocational and other qualifications that should be pursued by young people as part of any publicly funded programme;
- the QCA will rationalise by Autumn 2001 the plethora of qualifications up to A-level equivalent. We want all vocational qualifications to cover substantial programmes of work that add value to the skills and competence of learners; to reflect the sector specific needs of employment; to reach the high standards required by industry; and to provide a rich and solid base of practical and technical skills. It will be as clear as it is for academic education how each qualification fits into the overall framework.

2.26 We will develop vocational specialisation in further education. The Learning and Skills Council will invest £100 million over the next three years to develop specialisms, such as electronics, ICT or design and technology in further education colleges, for which they will be recognised as a centre of excellence locally, regionally or nationally. By 2004-05, 50 per cent of general further education colleges will have a specialism. They will offer tuition in their areas of expertise to technician level and the best will offer foundation degrees in partnership with universities. Colleges will work closely with employers to target provision on priority sectors. The drive for specialisation will ensure that colleges of further education teach vocational and technical education to the highest standards.

2.27 We will also create a new entitlement to a Modern Apprenticeship place for those young people who want to learn as they earn, and have the aptitude and ability for work-based learning. We will invest extra resources to increase the number of apprenticeships, ensuring that this expansion covers growth industries. Modern Apprenticeships for those aged 19 plus will be targeted on priority sectors to maximise value from our existing investment.

2.28 Standards in Modern Apprenticeships will be raised to match the best of apprenticeships amongst our competitors. A new Apprenticeship Diploma will provide a broader and better foundation of skills and knowledge than has been the case in the past – certifying knowledge and understanding, key skills and occupational specialisation at the appropriate level.

2.29 To ensure strong national leadership for apprenticeships, we will create a high level advisory committee, involving key business people, to advise on how standards can be kept consistently high, and to promote wide acceptance of apprenticeships.

2.30 For the first time there will be specific Standards Fund support for Apprenticeships: we will provide £15 million in 2002-03, rising to £25 million in 2003-04 to ensure colleges, private training providers and the highly effective group training associations all deliver to the highest standards.

> Simon undertook his Modern Apprenticeship at Taylor Bloxham Ltd, a large fine colour printers in Leicester. He worked on computers, taking a graphic designer's leaflet or booklet on disk and checking it was all correct and had appropriate photographs or images, before sending it to the platemakers to make it into plates for the printing process. He completed an NVQ Level 3 in Origination (processes which prepare original artwork/text for printing).
>
> Three years on, Simon says, "I am now a qualified digital operative working in Taylor Bloxham's pre-press department. I find my job thoroughly enjoyable and thrive on the challenge each job gives. If it wasn't for the training I received, my career wouldn't have been as rewarding."
>
> Speaking about Modern Apprenticeships, Emma Wixey, Taylor Bloxham's Human Resource Officer said, "We value the skills and knowledge a Modern Apprenticeship provides. It enables an apprentice to gain a good foundation in their chosen area whilst learning about the specific workflows within the department. The benefit of this is the combination of college based activities and hands on experience gained in the workplace."

Advanced ICT Skills and the High Tech Know-how to Match the Best of our Competitors

2.31 In the light of existing shortages in ICT skills, we face a major challenge to lever up these and other high tech skills in the workforce so that business is able to capitalise on the e-business revolution. We have already made significant progress in raising standards of basic ICT literacy. Today, 86 per cent of primary schools and 98 per cent of secondary schools are wired up to the Internet. In addition, an extra £1 billion for ICT over the next three years will help ensure that we achieve our proposed target for 2007 of 85 per cent of 14 year olds reaching level 5 or above in their Key Stage 3 tests in ICT.

2.32 We have also provided an 80 per cent discount on the cost of basic ICT courses for people opening Individual Learning Accounts. To date, over 58,000 have used their accounts to pay for ICT skills training. And to ensure that all adults have access to ICT skills, we will be introducing around 6,000 UK online centres in disadvantaged and rural communities by March 2002.

2.33 But we have much further to go in meeting the advanced ICT skills challenge. There are over 85,000 students on computer science courses in higher education – three times as many as there were a decade ago – and the launch of ICT related foundation degrees will add to the expansion. These developments will make a substantial contribution to expanding the supply of high tech skills. But as the *Skills for the Information Age* report has underlined, we need to go further and faster if we are to meet the challenge of new technologies. Our ambition is to make the UK the number one country for the supply of advanced ICT and related skills. This agenda must be demand-driven and we will work with business to ensure that demand is effectively articulated.

A people first economy

We will expand specialist ICT and other high tech learning programmes in our further and higher education system. A new, specialist focus on these skills is necessary if we are to increase the supply of skilled people to the levels we need. Courses will be provided at technician and first and post-graduate degree levels and will reflect a high level of business input into the curriculum. We will investigate how business can help deliver new learning programmes. By 2004-05 we will be training up to 10,000 students a year on full-time and updating courses. There will be new technology institutes described further in Chapter 3.

We will also increase significantly the number of unemployed people, those returning to the labour force, including lone parents, and people facing redundancy who acquire a basic ICT qualification. We will work with business to open new career paths in the ICT sector and will begin immediately by piloting within New Deal a programme to train 5,000 people over the next three years for technician jobs. In addition, we will improve the learning opportunities for unemployed and inactive people by increasing the use of innovative technology in assessment and careers guidance as well as basic and vocational skills training.

2.34 But our action plan must be broader than this if we are to ensure that we have a workforce with world class ICT skills. We will:

- support business to widen the pool of talent still further by bringing into skilled ICT employment those people facing disadvantage in the labour market, including people from ethnic minority communities, disabled people and older workers. We will work with business to introduce recruitment and retention practices that meet the needs of disadvantaged groups. We will support business efforts to create a more positive image of careers in high technology sectors that helps attract a more diverse workforce;
- work with business to reverse the serious under-representation of women in ICT jobs. We will identify global best practice that has helped women into ICT careers in other countries with a view to creating a more positive environment in the UK. Our aim is for the UK to match the best of our competitors with regard to women's employment in ICT;
- enable businesses to recruit more effectively and individuals to get the right job. We will map ICT qualifications and learning programmes against career paths in ICT, so that people can better understand what knowledge and skills they will need for different advanced ICT jobs. The QCA will create clear pathways through the qualification system by rationalising the very large number of ICT skills qualifications by 80 per cent. We will also work with business to develop the occupational framework for ICT that provides a common standard for describing ICT jobs and which represents a key business tool for assessing and improving skill levels;
- expand the number of advanced ICT teachers and open up new teaching opportunities to business experts. We will also work with business to help us in greatly increasing the opportunities for teachers in science, technology and engineering to undertake placements with companies. The further and higher education sectors will have substantial new resources to help recruit, retain and improve the effectiveness of teachers in shortage areas, such as ICT, where competition for staff is intense;
- ensure ICT students have the right practical skills and awareness of business. In partnership with business, we will increase the opportunities for students to gain relevant work experience. There will be particular emphasis on providing placements in which ICT students undertake short projects with local companies that are of value both to the companies and to the students themselves. There will be a special work experience programme for women. We will also support the further development and extension of Graduate Apprenticeships across the ICT and related high tech sectors.

2.35 These actions must be complemented by work in individual communities to promote ICT skills. Our strategy for community based initiatives will ensure that they encourage more people to join ICT training programmes and engage with local employers to encourage them to invest in ICT training.

2.36 We will continue to expand the use of ICT in the delivery of learning itself. The excellent progress we have made in improving computer/pupil ratios in schools will be maintained. Over the next three years, planned expenditure will enable us to reach a new target of 1:5 in secondary and 1:8 in primary schools by 2004. By 2002 all schools will have Internet access.

2.37 **learndirect** will be at the forefront of e-learning for adults, giving people easy access to learning opportunities at home, in the workplace and at **learndirect** learning centres nationwide. In further education, colleges will have access to a range of carefully focused learning materials which are being developed to support teaching and learning using ICT. Every college will be totally committed to the use of ICT as an integral part of its standards agenda. And we will invest £62 million over 2001-04 towards the new e-universities project, opening up online higher education to people who cannot attend a traditional campus.

The Cybrarian – "Virtual Librarian"

People who want to get to grips with the Internet can easily be turned off by its apparent complexity. This is doubly so for people with poor reading or computer handling skills or those with special educational needs or who have difficulty reading the screen.

To make the Internet more accessible to these people and others committed to lifelong learning and to give them greater confidence in using it, the Government is supporting the concept of Cybrarian, or Virtual Librarian.

This is a unique search and reference tool which delivers the text, pictures, audio or video material that the user wants directly to his or her personal computer, digital TV or mobile device. The key innovation is that the user can ask for information in a natural way, more akin to asking another person for assistance than to entering keywords in a conventional search engine. The Cybrarian can be fully incorporated into the UK online portal.

Investing In and Using the Skills and Talents of All

2.38 Too many firms still do not act on the knowledge that a higher skilled workforce would open up markets created by new technology and more sophisticated consumers. We still rely too heavily on highly skilled graduates, with business training catering best for those who are already well qualified and who work in large firms. Too many businesses also discriminate in their recruitment and employment practices against those from ethnic minority backgrounds, older workers, women or people who have disabilities. This is both unjust and self-defeating. In the modern economy, we need to utilise the skills and talents of all.

2.39 Our aim is to help employers drive up the skills of the workforce to match the best of our competitors, and get the best people with the relevant skills into the right jobs, so that businesses can expand into new markets and improve their productivity.

The Learning and Skills Council will set, with industry, clear targets for improving skills levels in the workforce. It will consult widely with business and other partners on targets and measurement in its draft workforce development strategy, which it will publish as a consultative document in June 2001. The strategy will also deal specifically with inequalities such as too little learning amongst part-time, low qualified or disabled workers and those from some ethnic groups.

We will create a strengthened sectoral skills focus through a reformed network of National Training Organisations. Over the next three years, we will invest an extra £45 million in a smaller, stronger network of National Training Organisations, with real authority and business leadership in their sectors. Each will be responsible for auditing sector skills needs, and designing and implementing initiatives to meet them. They will work closely with the Learning and Skills Council and with Regional Development Agencies on both planning and implementation.

Electroparts is one of a number of small firms which have benefited from the services of Electronics Yorkshire, an industry-led venture with the simple, but challenging, aim "To provide the region's electronics sector with the tools it needs to maximise its potential".

Electroparts is a small but growing company, formed in 1990 with two employees and currently employing fourteen. They provide a manufacturing facility for electrical and electronic sub-contract assembly, and plan to expand the business both in the UK and mainland Europe over the next five years, using the Internet as a key tool for trading and marketing their services. The technical and training resources available at Electronics Yorkshire are enabling Electroparts to diversify and refine their business and double their customer base over the next two to three years. Managing Director Carol Swallow says, "The facilities of Electronics Yorkshire have allowed us to train our people on new techniques and equipment, making sure we are ready to respond to the ever changing requirements of our customers, and providing the company with quality information to target our investment in equipment and resources."

2.40 Regional Development Agencies will have a key role to play in defining the skills needs in their regions in the context of their overall growth strategies. Their Skills Action Plans will be developed with local Learning and Skills Councils, and the National Training Organisations.

National Training Organisations can help businesses become more competitive. Skillset (Broadcast, Film, Video and Multimedia) has worked closely with film industry representatives and the Department for Culture, Media and Sport to provide an innovative solution – the Skills Investment Fund (SIF) – to the unique skills challenges facing the UK's film industry. Over 90 per cent of the film industry's workforce is freelance, with many companies hiring staff on a production by production basis. Funding the training of the growing number of freelances has become a priority for the industry. Contributions to the fund are voluntary and are raised on a percentage of the production budget of all UK film production intended for theatrical release.

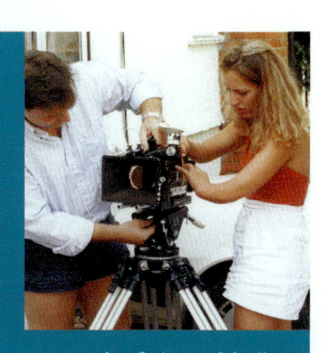

Within its first year the fund has attracted contributions of over £600,000 which has enabled Skillset to begin investment in a number of key priority areas identified by the industry. For example, January 2001 saw the first tranche of eight new entrants begin on a two year formal training scheme funded by the SIF. The SIF has also enabled the appointment of Skillset's new film advisor, the first sector specific appointment the National Training Organisation has made.

2.41 In addition to setting clearer targets and strengthening the peer influences on employers we will also tackle the key issues of raising training levels in small and medium sized enterprises and improving management skills. In particular, we will:

- help small and medium sized enterprises to spread the costs of training by supporting shared training arrangements and facilities, such as those provided by Group Training Associations. An extra £8 million will be spent to support these associations to provide Modern Apprenticeships in 2002-03 and 2003-04, along with access to funding such as the Small Firms Training Loan. The Learning and Skills Council will also work with the Small Business Service and **learndirect** to establish effective shared training networks nationwide. At the same time, the costs of learning will also be lowered through e-learning delivered by **learndirect**. **learndirect** will offer small businesses online learning through intermediaries such as the Small Business Service, directly through the network of **learndirect** centres, through mobile facilities, and through the **learndirect** website;
- work to improve leadership and management in the public and private sectors. The recommendations of the Council for Excellence in Management and Leadership will set an agenda for action to ensure that public and private training will better support management and leadership development;
- support a sustained campaign to convince companies that learning pays and that modern approaches to work organisation and management increase competitiveness. The Learning and Skills Council will speed progress towards the 2002 target of 10,000 small organisations and 45 per cent of medium and large organisations achieving Investors in People recognition.

A people first economy

> Investors in People (IiP) puts the development of people at the heart of business success. One third of the UK workforce work in organisations covered by Investors in People over 20,000 organisations, large and small, have achieved Investors in People status and are reaping the rewards through motivated and skilled staff. A further 22,000 are working towards Investors in People. Organisations recognised as Investors in People experience tangible benefits. A poll of over 2,000 recognised organisations found that 70 per cent had increased competitiveness, 70 per cent had increased productivity and 80 per cent had increased customer satisfaction.
>
> Enbray Cooper UK Limited – a leading British manufacturer of contactors serving the commercial, industrial and railway industries – has had to move into a bigger factory to cope with demand for its products. It has reached new markets all over the world following the development of a miniature contactor for electricity meters. Enbray Cooper's management give much of the credit to the firm's achievement of the Investors in People Standard. As plant manager Alan James says, "With the help of the Investors in People philosophy, Enbray has developed its teams through training to enable them to be flexible and adaptable to the changes in production methods that the new products will require."

2.42 Skills provide good earnings and secure employability, so the promotion of the skills of their members is a modern role for trade unions. Unions and workforce representatives have a crucial role to play in common cause with employers to ensure that individuals have the portable skills they need whilst meeting the immediate needs of business. We are committed as a Government to ensuring that Union Learning Representatives can play their part in both the competitiveness of the enterprise and the personal investment and gains for the individual employee from lifelong learning. These representatives, trained through a partnership between the TUC and Government, have been particularly successful in encouraging adults to learn who have not done any education or training since they left school.

We will consult on how to give statutory backing to the network of Union Learning Representatives. We will also promote a culture where employers and employees work together to create the best environment to realise the benefits of greater investment in skills through innovative projects supported under the Partnership Fund.

We will also work with National Training Organisations to test new, voluntary ways of funding training, including training loans that can be transferred between employers linked to the Small Firms Training Loans initiative. We will also use existing powers to provide statutory backing for proposals in any sector for collective skills funding arrangements, provided the social partners agree there is clear evidence of a skills deficit and that this is the best way forward.

2.43 Finally, we will provide practical, accessible help for businesses looking to recruit and retain a diverse workforce, and will raise awareness of the business case for equality at work. We will provide advice to employers, based on existing business experience, about introducing employment policies and practices geared towards work-life balance. We will expand the National Childcare Strategy in disadvantaged areas. We are also consulting on nearly 50 options to give more help to new parents and to the businesses that employ them, set out in our Green Paper, *Work and Parents: Competitiveness and Choice*.

2.44 The success of our strategy will require other partners to match the Government's commitment. Individuals must shoulder responsibilities to keep their skills up to date, and to be flexible and mobile in using those skills. Employers must recognise their competitive position increasingly rests on how they develop and use the skills of all their people. Companies must play a more active role in their own training programmes and collaborate with other companies to improve training in their locality or in their sector through National Training Organisations. They must also promote productivity through good relations at work. Education and training providers, such as colleges of further education, must develop deeper relationships with local businesses and more clearly address business needs.

> The Halifax believe that the diversity of their staff should reflect the communities in which they operate. Equal Opportunities adviser Tyrone Jones says, "This is a clear business issue – people tend to do business with like people." In the Bradford area, they formed an ethnic working party aimed at raising the profile of the Halifax as an equal opportunities employer; forging closer links with the local community; and, increasing customer service for ethnic minority customers. One of the Group's main ideas was to widen the skills of staff by training ethnic minority employees in recruitment administration, psychometric testing and interviewing. Prospective employees from ethnic communities now have contact with ethnic minority staff throughout the recruitment process, who understand their particular needs. The initiative has doubled ethnic minority representation in the Bradford area branches from 8 per cent to 16 per cent between 1999-2000 and has had a real impact for Asian customers – staff can speak a wider range of languages such as Urdu and Gujerati, and can act as interpreters for customers who speak little or no English.

3 All regions to prosper

A WHITE PAPER ON ENTERPRISE, SKILLS AND INNOVATION

Introduction

3.1 Ensuring that all parts and all people of the UK achieve their full potential is an economic as well as a social imperative. The way the economy is changing means there is a risk that success will come only in some regions and localities. We cannot accept that.

3.2 Strong regions and communities are a vital component of a strong national economy and open up greater opportunity for individual entrepreneurs and existing businesses. A strong national economy cannot function to its full capacity and individuals cannot realise their full potential if regions and localities are under performing.

3.3 We need a new approach to regional policy designed to build the capability of regions and communities. The new approach will be based on putting greater emphasis on growth within all regions and strengthening the building blocks for economic success by boosting regional capacity for innovation, enterprise and skills development. We must establish a sustained strategy to expand the winners' circle. We will also tackle the regeneration of deprived communities as set out in our action plan *A New Commitment to Neighbourhood Renewal*.

3.4 Regions where traditional manufacturing is important may be particularly exposed and we must help them to increase productivity and enable their businesses to move into higher value added products. The thrust of our new approach must be to enable more businesses, communities and individuals to anticipate and deal with change and restructuring and make the most of their talents and capabilities. We must also build on success and ensure that growth is not held back by infrastructure or skill constraints.

3.5 Government should not sit back and leave regional problems unthinkingly to the market. The causes of disparities between and within regions need to be addressed. Neither should it try to pick regional winners or subsidise failing businesses. Instead, Government must equip all regions and communities with the means to build on their own distinctive cultures, know-how and competitive advantages. This must be a bottom-up approach: the role of central Government must be to ensure that all regions and communities have the resources and capability to be winners. Strong regional policies have proved their worth in other European economies and in the USA.

3.6 The Government has already taken a number of important steps to address these issues in the regions. In particular the Regional Development Agencies have developed all embracing Regional Strategies for their regions. By covering employment, skills, innovation and regeneration, their strategies provide a coherent framework within which to decide how best to meet regional economic priorities. We have also focused Regional Selective Assistance in line with our new policy objectives, with around £250 million per year across Great Britain to lever in private investment and local Learning and Skills Councils, which will be operational from April 2001, will be responsible, working with business, for driving up skill levels in their areas.

3.7 The Regional Strategies reflect the differences between and within regions but they have all identified the importance of developing the skills base, encouraging enterprise and building a stronger capacity for innovation and technology transfer. This chapter shows how the Government will play its part in strengthening regional capabilities. It will:

- establish top class university innovation centres and new technology institutes in the regions to boost the levels of research and development, innovation and technology transfer and to provide the regions with the skills in ICT and high technology they need. The innovation centres and technology institutes will be closely linked to form a major network to encourage further development of business clusters and business incubators in the regions. They will create new dynamic hubs for growth;
- boost the capacity for enterprise in all regions by launching a new £75 million incubator fund to support new business formation: taking steps to ensure that the right support is available at the right time for small businesses that are committed to substantial growth and developing new early growth funding to fill gaps in the availability of small amounts of risk capital for new and growing businesses and those with intangible assets;
- support businesses and individuals in dealing with change by establishing a new Manufacturing Advisory Service to give special support to manufacturing industry; and
- promote the growth of successful clusters by asking the Regional Development Agencies to develop strategies for success for their regions, building on existing strengths, with the assistance of the clusters map published alongside this White Paper;
- remove unnecessary constraints to growth by improving transport and planning; and
- raise skills levels in deprived areas and communities and target help on businesses and people affected by restructuring and seeking new employment.

Our Goal

3.8 We do not intend to hold back any region – we must ensure that all prosper. Our goal is to increase the rate of growth in all regions by addressing under-performance and building on success. There is no single solution that can be applied across the UK. The Regional Development Agencies, together with local Learning and Skills Councils and the work of Government Offices, provide a channel for flexible policies to meet the different needs of regions and communities and ensure equal opportunities for all. We will encourage regional partnerships to ensure policies and services for business are properly joined up.

Where the UK Stands

3.9 All parts of the UK are benefiting from the stable macroeconomic environment. 1.1 million more people are in work than in 1997. Unemployment is at its lowest rate since the mid-1970s.

3.10 However, there are large disparities between and within regions and in certain disadvantaged areas. Since 1990, the share of output in the UK has declined noticeably in the North East, West Midlands, Wales and Scotland and increased in the Eastern Region, London and the South East.

3.11 There are also significant variations in the extent to which regions possess the key building blocks for economic success. In 1997, investment by manufacturing business in R&D represented 12 per cent of gross value added in the South East, compared with 1.8 per cent in Yorkshire and the Humber, 2.9 per cent in the North East and 4.7 per cent in the North West. In 1999, there were 66 new business registrations for every 10,000 adults in London and 45 in the South East, compared with 29 in Yorkshire and the Humber, and just 21 in the North East. In the North East and the West Midlands almost 20 per cent of the working age population had no qualifications compared to 11 per cent in the South East. The South East with 32 per cent of the population of VAT registered businesses has 46 per cent of England's venture capital backed companies, while the South West with 11 per cent of the population has six per cent.

3.12 The UK also has some very strong clusters of economic growth and innovation. Particularly successful examples are financial services in the South East, high technology industries in Cambridge and Oxford, a range of creative industries in London, and information technology along the M4 corridor. There are also important chemical industry clusters in a number of regions and significant embryonic clusters such as biomedical industries in the North West, leisure software in Yorkshire and the Humber and environmental industries in the West Midlands. However, some of these areas risk becoming victims of their own success by running up against constraints in terms of, for example, transport infrastructure, land use and skills shortages.

What the Government will do

Building Regional Capacity for Innovation, Skills and R&D

3.13 The role of our universities in the economy is crucial. They are powerful drivers of innovation and change in science and technology, the arts, humanities, design and other creative disciplines. They produce people with knowledge and skills; they generate new knowledge and import it from diverse sources; and they apply knowledge in a range of environments. They are also the seedbed for new industries, products and services and are at the hub of business networks and industrial clusters of the knowledge economy.

3.14 For businesses to grow and succeed, it is essential for them to have access to world class research and development and skills. We must transform their capacity to exploit the opportunities of new technology and sustain a diversified economic base. However, private sector R&D is low in some regions, there are gaps in the skills of the workforce and the potential of universities to act as hubs of growth is not fully realised. All the Regional Development Agencies recognise the importance of building effective links between universities and businesses in their regions.

3.15 Through imaginative partnerships between universities and business we can stimulate new investment in research and development and new high tech skills. We can also give a major boost to transferring technology to business. Through colleges we can ensure that the flow of skills and know-how reaches into the wider community, and through exploitation of intellectual property rights, ensure a reward for creativity.

We will establish university innovation centres. These will be top class, long term research partnerships between major business interests and the university sector. They will create new dynamic links for growth. They will be at the heart of cluster development and support for new start-ups and businesses that are growing in business incubators. Through them, businesses will be able to make the most of the specialist knowledge that is available regionally.

We will also take decisive action to boost the supply of high tech skills including multi-media and link this with the transfer of expertise to local small businesses. We will establish new technology institutes based on partnerships between universities, colleges and local business. They will provide specialist ICT and other high tech learning programmes and will work closely with local companies to ensure they have the know-how to apply advanced technology practices. They will also help to cascade skills and know-how to the wider community.

3.16 The university innovation centres and technology institutes will form a major new network, based in every region, to boost the level of research and development, innovation and technology transfer and to provide regions with the skills in ICT and high technology they need. The network will be driven forward by a partnership involving DTI, the Higher Education Funding Council for England (HEFCE), the Learning and Skills Council, the Small Business Service and the Regional Development Agencies. They will all come together to lend their resources and expertise to ensuring the most effective networks and hubs of growth are established within and across regions. DTI will work together with DfEE, through the resources allocated to the HEFCE, to develop the network.

3.17 We are able to announce today the setting up of five university innovation centres. We will encourage the setting up of further university innovation centres from a range of funds including the Higher Education Innovation Fund, where an additional £80 million over the next three years was announced in the Spending Review to strengthen business/higher education partnerships. Loans from the European Investment Bank could also be used to help fund the centres. The Bank has decided to provide additional funds for investment in research and development by industry across the EU, of which £250 million is expected to be lent to UK companies over the next three years. The EIB is also considering a new £100 million loan facility for investment in universities. This is being discussed with HEFCE for implementation later this year.

3.18 An example of a new collaborative research venture is the partnership in information and communication technologies that has been established between BT and University College London, with support from Agilent, Corning Communications, Marconi, and Nortel. The centre for research and associated postgraduate training will be established with the collaboration of BTexaCT, BT's advanced communication technologies business, and based at its Adastral.Park site near Ipswich. It will support a community of around 50 researchers focusing on the technological development needs of industrial partners and fostering closer co-operation between academics and industry.

3.19 The five new regionally based projects announced today will build on this type of good practice. A total of £30 million will be available to support collaborative R&D and knowledge transfer activity. Each project is focused on a sector recognised as being of strategic importance to the region and will emphasise the importance of large companies as well as the small businesses in their supply chains collaborating with academics for competitive advantage.

All regions to prosper

3.20 The five projects are:

- microsystems and nanotechnology in the North East, involving BAE SYSTEMS and Procter & Gamble, with the stated intention of using the research excellence of Durham and Newcastle universities in this field to give a technological lead to existing instrumentation and bioscience businesses, and to catalyse the growth of a new industrial cluster in the region;
- an organic chemicals project in the North West involving a number of international companies, including Astra Zeneca, Avecia, UCB Films and Unilever aimed at ensuring that university research, particularly in the collaborative Manchester Polymer Centre, is focused on improving the performance of the region's existing chemical industry and helping to establish new product lines in existing firms and spawn new startup companies;
- communications, computing and content technologies in the South West, centred on the University of Bristol and involving companies such as Hewlett Packard, STMicroelectonics and Broadcom and intended to unite key industrial and academic research capabilities to provide a competitive response to the convergence of these fields;
- business to business e-commerce in the West Midlands involving Marconi, Sun Microsystems and the Parametric Technology Corporation, recognising that e-business is radically changing how organisations communicate, co-operate and make decisions, and that it is essential to prepare businesses for this new environment; and
- aerospace manufacturing in Yorkshire, centred on a new Technology Park in Sheffield under the leadership of Sheffield University and involving the Boeing Company, the Hamble Group, Technicut and a number of other research organisations and companies from throughout the aerospace components supply chain.

3.21 All the projects are intended to serve as exemplars to inspire similar projects in other sectors and regions. Some, such as that in the West Midlands involving Marconi and the Warwick Manufacturing Group, extend existing collaborative relationships.

3.22 Our aim is to establish up to two new technology institutes in each region. They will involve universities working with local colleges and small groups of businesses. They will provide courses mainly at technician level but also including foundation, first and post graduate degree level. The institutes will bring together teaching and skills development with work to support the transfer of new technologies and business practices to companies. This will involve exchanges of staff between institutes, business work experience placements for students and training sessions delivered on site with companies. Universities and colleges, working in partnership with leading IT companies, will be invited to bid for funding for the new technology institutes. The funding will be administered jointly by the Higher Education Funding Council for England and the Learning and Skills Council.

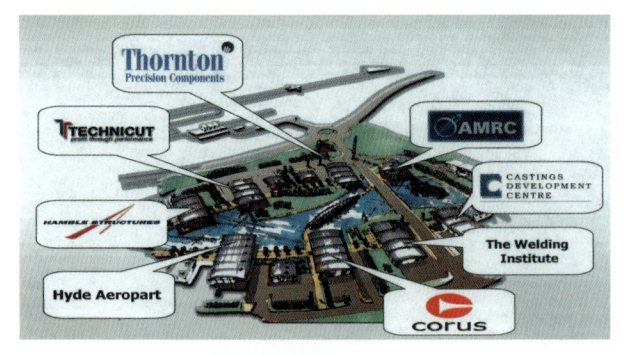

South Yorkshire Aerospace Cluster: led by the University of Sheffield and The Boeing Company.

3.23 Reading College and School of Art and Design is a good example of the sort of collaboration we wish to develop through the new technology institutes. It provides the core of a regional partnership for e-learning through a virtual college providing online high technology and advanced IT skills to the SME sector. It works closely with Thames Valley University and Oxford Brookes University. Its Digital Academy brings together industry, further education and higher education on programmes ranging from web-page design, computer animation and multimedia technology to digital printing and electronic publishing.

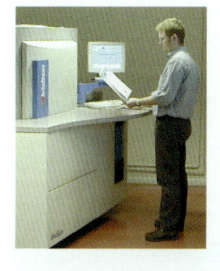

Leeds College of Technology

Leeds College of Technology is at the leading edge of skills development for the print industry. Twenty per cent of the UK's printing industry is located in the North of England and the college aims to encourage young people to enter the industry by offering specially developed customised courses. The centre has secured over £2 million of private sponsorship from companies including Heidelberg, Komori, Xerox and Agfa. The Print Media Centre's membership scheme encourages companies and individuals with an interest in the print industry to participate in the centre's programmes. Employer feedback helps the college ensure that its provision keeps pace with digital and electronic advances in industry. The college is in partnership with two major universities in Leeds and will become a printing sector centre for **learndirect**, which complements its online training provision for the engineering manufacturing and motor vehicles industries.

Encouraging Enterprise – New Business Formation

3.24 Small businesses are a key engine of the economy. They provide about half of all employment and that proportion is growing. There is already work in progress across Government towards creating the right environment for encouraging enterprise. The Global Entrepreneurship Monitor 2000 identified that the participation of women in entrepreneurship is critical to long term economic prosperity. Women currently start up only a third of businesses in the UK. There are many potential entrepreneurs amongst women and other under-represented groups and action will be taken to remove any particular barriers to starting up in business and in promoting enterprise to these groups through the provision of business support and incubator space. We need to ensure that all entrepreneurs are able to achieve their full potential. Not all new start-ups and small firms will want to grow substantially but it is vital that we do everything we can to help those that do. Business incubation where start-ups are able to work within a supportive environment during the early stages of their development, is a key regional priority for many of the Regional Development Agencies.

3.25 A supportive environment for new businesses offered by business incubators including flexible leases, good communications, mentoring and business advice has been shown to help start-ups survive and prosper. 80 per cent of businesses that start in such incubators are still in business after five years, compared with only 33 per cent which do not have such support. A number of incubators have been developed particularly for high tech start-ups and specialist clusters. For example, the East of England Development Agency is developing two new incubators – one specialising in telecommunications and another in North Sea oil and gas energy industries. And in the North West, the Regional Development Agency's Business Incubation Programme will establish eleven high tech startup businesses within the clusters identified in the Regional Strategy. However, supply is not meeting demand and there is a shortage of workspace providing incubation for those wanting to startup in their local community.

All regions to prosper

To encourage business formation and growth in all regions, we will launch a new £75 million incubator fund operated by the Small Business Service. Particular attention will be paid to meeting the needs of women and other under-represented groups.

3.26 The Small Business Service will fund, with other finance providers, the development of additional incubators within local communities to help ensure that all start-up companies likely to benefit from such facilities have the chance to do so, and to draw on their access to expertise appropriate to each business. The bidding process will be managed at regional level by the RDAs on behalf of the SBS. The aim is to develop around 75 incubators by 2004. We expect around 30 to 35 businesses to be helped by each incubator, enabling a total of around 2,500 companies to be helped at any one time.

3.27 The new fund will support the creation of incubator space, refurbishment of workspace to provide a more supportive environment and the linking of business support and workspace provision with other infrastructure such as broadband communications networks. The Small Business Service will work with Regional Development Agencies and local partners to ensure that a full range of incubation facilities is available in a region to assist in cluster development and regeneration. The European Investment Bank is considering a new facility of up to £75 million to support the incubator fund to be operated by the Small Business Service.

Wandsworth Youth Enterprise

Wandsworth Youth Enterprise business incubation programme provides intensive support specifically designed to help young people aged 17-30 start-up and run a successful enterprise. A client-led counselling service is interlinked with business skills workshops, training courses and managed workspace provision with 25 subsidised business units. The average survival rate has been 85-90 per cent trading after two years. Over 3,000 young people have been helped under this scheme which was set up to tackle problems of unemployment, social exclusion and lack of opportunities for young people in an area of high unemployment and a diverse multicultural community.

Encouraging Enterprise – Support for Growth Businesses

3.28 Estimates suggest that about 12 per cent of small and medium sized businesses are committed to substantial growth as a key business objective. The aim is to network to help those companies access the support and advice they need from both the public and private sectors.

3.29 We need these businesses to grow, however identifying them can be difficult. But a number of Government organisations such as the Inland Revenue, Customs & Excise and the Employment Service are well placed to identify companies which are growing quickly, because they know when companies reach particular employee or turnover thresholds. The Small Business Service will therefore work with these bodies to ensure that growth companies are aware of the opportunity to work with Business Link operators in order to access the support they need. Business Links will stand ready to offer whatever support is needed and deliver this in a manner appropriate to the business needs. We will, for instance, ensure our support is marketed to all sectors including the creative industries which have, to date, been reluctant to use traditional business support mechanisms. While each firm's requirements will be different, the kind of support and advice likely to be available in the package of support will include:

- access to finance including risk capital, to ensure the firm has the resources it needs to grow;
- effective access to information and communication technologies to help widen their markets;
- advice on how to accelerate and continue product and process innovation development to help the firm go beyond being a single product/process company;
- information and advice on trading overseas; and
- advice on how to manage growth effectively since many small firms stutter as they go beyond owner-manager status.

3.30 Lack of management skills and expertise can often hold back growth companies. The local Learning and Skills Council will work closely with employers and their sector based National Training Organisations to identify skills needs and bring together like-minded employers, particularly in small firms, to share resources and develop joint action plans. Close links between the Learning and Skills Council and the Small Business Service will be important in delivering these improvements.

3.31 It is also highly desirable that larger companies play a role in the development of growing businesses. For example, the Small Business Service is currently developing with BAE SYSTEMS a programme under which a number of their senior executives would serve as non-executive directors or mentors of growth orientated small companies. This would contribute to the personal development of those individuals by giving them a fresh perspective on the business issues facing smaller companies, while allowing the smaller companies to gain the benefit of external advice from potential 'high-flyers' with BAE SYSTEMS. This is currently being developed as a pilot programme, but if it proves successful, the Small Business Service will seek to widen this initiative into a 'Business Buddies' scheme and involve more companies both large and small.

Encouraging Enterprise – Widening Access to Finance

3.32 Despite the growth of formal and informal venture capital, not all businesses with growth potential can get the risk capital they need. Venture capital investment in the UK in 1999 exceeded £6 billion, more than double the amount in 1997 and involving £4 billion in management buyouts. Between 1998 and 1999 investment in start-ups rose by 15 per cent and in early stage companies by 24 per cent, with the development of new seed funds (particularly in technology sectors) and a more active business angel market.

3.33 Nonetheless, a number of independent reports, including a recent IPPR report on this issue, have confirmed that it can still be difficult to raise small amounts of risk capital, particularly for investment in intangibles such as R&D and in the creative industries. Institutional investors tend to favour private equity over classic venture capital. So new knowledge companies, as well as more traditional forms, need a little extra help.

To encourage more start-ups and growth firms, we will develop with the Small Business Service and the private sector new early growth funding for start-ups and smaller growing businesses. This funding will help to meet the need for small amounts of risk capital. We will aim to help a minimum of 1,000 businesses over the next three years committing up to £50 million from the Enterprise Fund.

3.34 We will develop new funding streams to help plug the financing gap for start-ups and small growing firms. We will target businesses seeking to raise up to £50,000, including innovative and knowledge-intensive businesses, as well as businesses such as smaller manufacturers needing fresh investment to pursue new opportunities. We will consult with banks and the private finance industry in the first half of 2001 to design an effective new public/private partnership, consistent with EU rules on assistance to small firms. Funding will be stimulated through new guarantee or co-funding mechanisms and the costs will be met from the Enterprise Fund.

All regions to prosper

3.35 To ensure regional availability of finance, we are working with the European Investment Bank through the European Investment Fund to promote the accessibility of venture capital in all regions. Subject to EU approval and private co-investor support, we hope to have the first of the network of Regional Venture Capital Funds making investments later this year.

3.36 The Government has welcomed the Social Investment Task Force report, published in October 2000, which recommended a five-point action plan for increasing private investment in enterprises in disadvantaged areas. In response, the Government is:
- due to consult shortly on the proposed Community Investment Tax Credit;
- working closely with the venture capital industry to set up the first Community Development Venture Fund;
- encouraging banks to disclose their individual lending activities to firms in under-invested areas;
- due to issue guidance, through the Charities Commision, on how charities can invest in social enterprises, for example through "programme-related investment"; and
- encouraging the community development sector to form an effective trade association, and considering the proposal for a community development "champion".

3.37 The Government has also set up the £100 million Phoenix Fund, which is run by the Small Business Service. This seeks to encourage enterprise among those who are less likely to participate, such as people living in disadvantaged neighbourhoods, women, people with disabilites, and ethnic minorities. The fund promotes the provision of good quality business support, including projects giving access to business funding for those who find this difficult to obtain from conventional sources. The first successful bidders, some 50 organisations involving projects worth £15 million, were announced on 5th February 2001. Further rounds of bidding are scheduled later this year.

Dealing with Change – Manufacturing Excellence

3.38 An innovative, high value added manufacturing sector is a vital part of the economy. Manufacturing directly employs four million people and accounts for almost £150 billion of output per year. A further 2.5 million service sector jobs depend on manufacturing through supply chain linkages. Many of our most innovative businesses are manufacturers investing heavily in research and development. We need more world class manufacturers.

3.39 We need to encourage more manufacturers to follow the example of the best but some small manufacturers lack the resources to move their performance beyond the level needed for day to day survival. To help them adopt current best manufacturing practices they need a convenient, easily available and affordable source of advice on technology, manufacturing operations and training issues. The stress on the importance of manufacturing and the need to update the competitiveness of the manufacturing base is a key priority for many of the Regional Development Agencies. For example in the West Midlands the Regional Development Agency is building on the work of the Rover Task Force and has set out a wide range of linked, priority actions to deliver a step change in the region's economy.

To help such businesses we will establish a new Manufacturing Advisory Service in partnership with the Regional Development Agencies, to provide practical help with new manufacturing technology. DTI will provide £15 million over three years to complement funding from the Regional Development Agencies and the Welsh Development Agency.

3.40 The new service will be designed to work alongside other programmes, such as those developed in the West Midlands. It will be delivered in concert with the Small Business Service with initial access normally being via Business Links and draw on successful experience from the USA. It will comprise:

- regional centres for manufacturing excellence, which will provide practical advice and assistance on a wide range of manufacturing issues through teams of experts available to diagnose problems and provide tailored solutions for individual firms. The Regional Development Agencies and Welsh Development Agency will progressively establish regional centres from the second half of the year;
- a supporting national network to ensure manufacturers in all regions can have access to the best quality expertise. The first phase of the national network will be operational by summer 2001 and form part of the Business Link Information and Advice Service.

3.41 In addition, we are developing further partnerships to build on the successful SMMT Industry Forum Programme in the vehicle industry. The programme is delivering hard, measurable results including *"right first time"* quality increased by two thirds, productivity doubled and stock turns more than trebled. A further five partnerships have already been launched, covering aerospace, ceramics, chemicals, metals and oil and gas; one for textiles and clothing is being established: and we aim to extend support to four more sectoral partnerships. All these activities will contribute to the CBI-led Fit for the Future national best practice campaign to help more companies achieve world class performance.

3.42 The Government will also extend the programme of Faraday partnerships that link universities, independent research organisations and firms to bring new products and processes in key industrial sectors to market more quickly. Ten partnerships are already established in sectors such as new materials, sensors and food process engineering. They employ people who can interpret the findings of research for business and carry the needs of business back into the research communities. We will launch another eight partnerships in April 2001; and issue a call for proposals in May 2001 to expand the network to at least 24 partnerships by 2002. Whereas university innovation centres will focus on regional-scale links with a strategically important grouping of companies and build on the physical presence of a major research capability, the Faraday partnerships promote a broader base of many organisations working together in a nationally important sector.

3.43 We will continue to support LINK programmes which encourage businesses to work with the research base in universities and elsewhere. For example, the Foresight Vehicle programme is developing a growing network of 400 organisations and a research portfolio worth over £75 million to date. And the new LINK Bioremediation Programme will open for proposals from April to promote biotechnology for environmental clean up. The DTI is committing £2 million to this programme with over £5 million from other government sponsors including several research councils and the Environment Agency.

3.44 There is a growing demand in universities and research labs for people who can work at the interface between research and the commercial world, identifying technology that has commercial value and managing the exploitation process. The Government intends to work with interested bodies and universities to review how best to stimulate the provision of training in this field.

All regions to prosper

Clusters and Strategies for Success

3.45 The Government is working with the Regional Development Agencies to identify the distribution and nature of clusters in the UK. The Clusters Report *UK Business Clusters: A First Assessment* identifies over 150 manufacturing and service clusters around the UK. Some of these are highly successful, others embryonic, while others may need to increase their rate of innovation and move into higher value added products if they are to play a major role in the knowledge economy. Examples of new clusters include environmental industries in the North East and Yorkshire and the Humber; Biomedical supplies in the North West and speciality chemicals in the North East and North West.

To remove constraints and highlight the potential for growth of successful clusters, the Government has asked Regional Development Agencies to produce strategies for success for their regions, drawing on their regional strategies and using information such as the clusters map to identify further potential centres of growth.

3.46 The Regional Development Agencies have produced Regional Economic Strategies and associated Innovation Strategies and are already working with local authorities and other key partners to support many of these clusters and identify opportunities for new development. The strategies will also provide a strong co-ordinating framework for the work of the local Learning and Skills Councils and will inform their plans for education and training at local level.

3.47 The clusters report provides a systematic basis for this work and identifies clusters of international and national as well as regional significance. An example is the work by Yorkshire Forward, the Regional Development Agency in Yorkshire and the Humber, which has already resulted in a number of centres of excellence being set up for chemicals, food, construction, printing, electronics, multimedia, textiles and medical equipment.

3.48 Other examples of Agency activity are in the East Midlands where the Regional Development Agency aims to identify emerging clusters around the region and recruit innovation champions to facilitate development of the clusters. Using a similar approach, the Agency in the North East aims to develop an information hub to encourage greater collaboration and sharing of best practice between clusters. In the North East current activity is focussed around existing clusters, including chemicals, electronics and automotive, and developing clusters, including speciality chemicals, nanotechnology, tourism and cultural industries. A range of activities are now being taken forward to support these existing and emerging clusters including the establishment of the Northern Film and Media Office to provide a platform for the focussed development of the multimedia and film industries in the region. And in the South West a number of initiatives are being taken forward including facilities for high tech businesses linked to an emerging biotechnology cluster around Porton Down and Exeter Innovation Centre. Further examples of Regional Development activity to support clusters are described in the box opposite.

3.49 Drawing on this material, the Agencies will now develop strategies for success. They will explore in more detail opportunities for reinforcing success and addressing growth pressures within their regions.

3.50 All the Agencies will also spread good practice and foster collaboration and connections between these networks and clusters. Under their new funding arrangements, they will have more flexibility in spending their overall budgets to address problems in growth areas.

All regions to prosper

Examples of Regional Development Agency Cluster Development Activity

Motorsport

The motorsport industry makes a major contribution to the UK economy in terms of GDP and is a source of international expertise as well as high tech employment. Around 70 per cent of the industry in the UK is located within the boundaries of the South East England Development Agency, East of England Development Agency, East Midlands Development Agency and Advantage West Midlands. The Agencies have been working together with the Motorsport Industry Association (MIA) to promote the sector and maintain its international expertise.

The Regional Development Agencies are working with the MIA to capitalise on supply chain linkages, to facilitate technology transfer and the diffusion of innovation in the fields of performance engineering and materials, and to exploit the commercial spin-offs achievable through greatly increased marketing, merchandising and tourism links. Plans for a national training network and advanced engineering centre are also well advanced.

Bionow

Biotechnology (particularly biomedicine) is an emerging cluster in the North West. It builds directly on the region's significant strengths in its universities, research institutes and teaching hospitals, a large and established pharmaceutical and chemicals sector, and a growing community of biotechnology companies.

Led by the North West Development Agency the initiative now involves more than 300 individuals and companies. It has organised two inward missions from the USA and attendance at BIO 2000 (Boston) and BioJapan 2000 (Tokyo). It has also started to provide strategic support for three particular projects relating to biomanufacture, bioinformatics and core technology development.

In the last year 18 new biotechnology companies have been established or moved into the region.

Removing Barriers to Growth

3.51 In many areas of the country, growth is creating pressure on the local environment and infrastructure. Action is needed to build on success and remove barriers to growth, through improvements in infrastructure as well as assisting the development of innovative networks and clusters.

To help remove some of the constraints experienced by businesses in high growth localities we are making the planning system quicker and more efficient, and improving the regional and local transport infrastructure.

Improving Transport and Planning

3.52 Efficient transport is the backbone of the national and regional economy. We have announced the biggest programme of transport investment ever seen in *Transport 2010: The Ten Year Plan* which will modernise and improve this country's transport networks. We will be spending £180 billion over the next ten years including £60 billion on railways, £59 billion on local transport, £21 billion on the strategic road network, and £25 billion in London.

3.53 The first schemes under the Plan are now coming forward at local level and we have just announced the first instalment of our new capital investment in local transport. Local authorities will spend £8.4 billion over the next five years on measures contained within their strategic local transport plans. Studies are also under way to tackle the most severe of the congestion problems across England. The Government is committed under the Ten Year Transport Plan to fund the schemes which emerge from these studies. In London, the Mayor who has responsibility for transport will issue a transport strategy in July 2001.

3.54 The improvements delivered by the Ten Year Plan as a whole will increase productivity and cut business costs by making journeys quicker and more reliable, both for freight and passengers. With inputs from the new regional transport strategies, they will improve access for people and goods in all parts of the country, so that all regions can meet their full potential.

3.55 There is a lot business itself can do to also help tackle transport problems. Through our Sustainable Distribution Strategy, Government is helping industry ensure efficient supply chains, and at a local level we are facilitating businesses to implement, and gain the benefits from, more environmentally sustainable travel patterns for their employees.

3.56 As well as facilitating major infrastructure, we also need an efficient planning system which provides prompt decisions about proposed business investment. The record of local authorities in dealing quickly and efficiently with planning applications is variable and we will be using the local Government Best Value regime to tackle the poorest performing planning authorities so that they improve significantly their handling of planning applications.

3.57 We have set out our expectations of the planning system in a concordat with the Local Government Association (LGA). The Confederation of British Industry (CBI), other business bodies and the voluntary sector followed up with a "planning users" concordat. Separate agreements have been issued or are in preparation, including one prepared by the East Midlands Regional Development Agency. We shall be encouraging other regions to follow suit.

3.58 We are also promoting increased efficiency in the handling of planning applications. One way is by extending the use of electronic processing of planning cases within government. We are setting up a £3 million project to provide an Internet Planning Portal as a single access point to the planning service.

3.59 Regional planning bodies are working with the Regional Development Agencies and business to ensure an integrated approach to development at the regional level. This is where the Agencies' economic strategies come together with regional planning guidance and regional transport strategies. We want business to be better engaged with the preparation of these strategies and in development plans at local level.

3.60 The planning system needs to underpin development of business clusters. Guidance has already been issued to local authorities relating to planning for clusters at both regional and local level. An example is the new Regional Planning Guidance for East Anglia, which requires local planning authorities, working with the Regional Development Agency and other regional partners, to identify suitable locations for research and technology-based industries and their support services. The objective is to extend the clusters based around Cambridge to other parts of the region.

Overcoming the Skills Divide

3.61 Low skills are a real barrier to economic development. Low-skilled communities have high rates of unemployment, and of low-paid employment, and low skills discourage companies from locating and investing in communities. Conversely, where skill levels are high, and where vocational education and training provided by colleges and other institutions is flexible and meets the needs of potential employers, communities can attract and retain investment and have the resilience to adapt to the swift pace of change in the modern labour market.

3.62 With business people forming 40 per cent of the membership of its local councils, the Learning and Skills Council gives us an unprecedented opportunity to ensure that education and training meets the needs of local businesses. Working with Regional Development Agencies it will provide up to date intelligence on regional and local skill needs and will target areas with a low skills base and those with recruitment difficulties. The new specialist centres of vocational excellence, based in further education colleges, which will be co-ordinated by the Council will have a key role in meeting the skill pressures facing local firms.

3.63 Community Champions is a good example of an initiative which empowers local people to find sustainable solutions they know will work. It aims to help people build on skills they already have and encourage them to help others become more involved in community and regeneration activity. We are providing £3 million from the Active Community Fund to extend this scheme. We are also providing £13.5 million from this fund and matched funding from the Higher Education Funding Council for England to enable students and staff in higher education institutions to engage in volunteer work with their local communities.

3.64 The work of the Learning and Skills Council in raising skill levels in deprived communities fits closely with the development of skills under the New Deal. Later this year we will enhance the New Deal for those aged 25 and over. Extra help will be given to everyone who has been unemployed for more than 18 months and, for people between ages 25-50, we will make the New Deal compulsory. We will ensure that we are reaching the hardest to help and tackling skill shortages by making the New Deal more flexible and responsive to the needs of individuals and employers.

3.65 The Council has a clear remit to help in building the capacity of people living in deprived neighbourhoods and to promote equality and social inclusion. It will use the Local Initiatives Fund to develop a wider range of learning opportunities in these neighbourhoods. It will help provide training for community leaders and groups involved in self-help projects. In line with the Action Plan to implement the National Strategy for Neighbourhood Renewal the Council will help to bridge the gap between deprived communities and the rest of the country by helping to build the self-confidence of these communities and engaging the wider community in learning.

All regions to prosper

3.66 We will press ahead with action to bridge the digital divide. We are investing £252 million to establish UK Online centres in our most disadvantaged communities. We are also investing £10 million through the Wired Up Communities Initiative to test how making ICT available to people in our most disadvantaged communities enables them to develop skills, enhances work prospects and supports community regeneration. We will begin phase 2 projects under the Wired Up Communities Initiative in July this year and we will increase the number of UK Online centres to 6000 by 2004. Both these initiatives will drive forward our strategy to provide access to ICT and the Internet to all who want it.

3.67 The low skills base of many communities is partly a result of low attainment in formal education, and low rates of continuing education. Education Action Zones and the Excellence in Cities initiative are helping to combat underachievement in deprived communities. In addition Education Maintenance allowances are strengthening the incentives to young people to stay on in learning. Through the Excellence Challenge programme we will bring higher education and further education into both Education Action Zones and the Excellence in Cities partnerships to start working with able young people from age 13 from disadvantaged backgrounds. The programme will provide information and practical support for young people, their teachers and parents about the opportunities and benefits of higher education.

SEEDA Bursary Scheme

SEEDA, the Regional Development Agency in the South East, has launched a rolling programme funding postdoctoral fellows in South East higher education institutions to investigate skills shortages for the knowledge economy.

The scheme, managed by the South East Higher Education (HE) regional consortium, and supported by Skills Insight, the regional skills observatory and SEEDA sector groups, will develop a detailed understanding of future skills needs in specific sectors and ensure these are fully understood and acted upon by the region's HE research base.

The first three bursaries focus on the Media & Creative, Marine Technology and Tourism sectors, involving the Surrey Institute of Art & Design, Southampton Institute and the University of Brighton.

Further bursaries will follow so that a cadre of researchers and their supervisors will be built to act as an academic 'future think tank'. By working in the research environment they will be able to identify growth points for new industries and therefore anticipate future skills needs.

Dealing with Change – Major Restructuring

3.68 Relocations, rationalisations and redundancies happen as the economy changes in response to globalisation, shifts in consumer preferences and new technology. These changes cannot be stopped or reversed, but people and communities need support from Government so they can anticipate change, adapt and move forward. Macroeconomic stability and a supportive business environment will foster the growth of new firms and new jobs throughout the economy. On occasions the pace and extent of change means communities need more focused support.

3.69 The kind of support needed will vary but could include fostering more business start-ups; facilitating the preparation and release of sites for new investment; help for supply chains; and advice on diversification and new markets.

3.70 Existing Government programmes are already available to help and the Regional Development Agencies and the Employment Service have the responsibility to co-ordinate resources at the regional level.

In addition, to enable communities and individuals affected by redundancy to find the right jobs more quickly, and growing companies to tackle skill shortages we are creating a new Job Transition Service building on the help already available through the Employment Service.

3.71 The new Job Transition Service is designed to not only help individuals and their families cope with job loss, but also to support employers who need help to recruit people with the right skills for their business. It will provide all those affected by a major redundancy with a personal adviser who will assess each individual's employability in the local labour market, focusing on transferable skills and those skills required by new employers. Personal advice on finance, self-employment, access to training courses and future career options will be offered to every individual who may need access to existing programmes or new funding in order to develop skills appropriate to the changing needs of the local labour market.

3.72 The new Service will:
- give people at local level power to decide the best approach for them and their community and help them to put it into practice;
- reduce the impact of redundancies on the whole community by more flexible and discretionary deployment of the current Rapid Response Fund. The help will extend to partners of those made redundant, as well as others in the community affected indirectly;
- be 'demand led', working with potential employers to analyse their skills needs and matching them against available recruits and running skill development programmes to close the gap; and
- ensure that the jobs people move into offer opportunities for progression, through structured training including support for apprentice-style programmes for those wishing to change their career.

3.73 The new service is being developed with the help of those on the ground who are dealing with recent major redundancies. Working with partners, we will ensure that the service reflects the needs of individuals and employers rather than the assumptions of central government.

All regions to prosper

4 Investing in new sources of business success

A WHITE PAPER ON ENTERPRISE, SKILLS AND INNOVATION

Introduction

4.1 Economic growth and increased productivity are driven by innovation – the process of turning ideas into new products and services. For businesses, innovation creates better products, delivered faster and more efficiently. In competitive markets, businesses which fail to innovate will be left behind.

4.2 Innovation depends on the skills, knowledge, creativity and enterprise of individuals working in business and research. Government also has a role to play. It can help drive innovation by promoting an environment where competition works well and successful innovators are rewarded. It can invest to ensure that the infrastructure and research networks are in place to open up opportunities to innovate. It can accelerate the process of innovation by promoting the sharing and exploitation of new knowledge, particularly between science and industry.

4.3 Economic success will depend on effectively exploiting the emerging sources of innovation. Recent scientific advances in genomics, e-science and environmental technologies give us outstanding opportunities not just to create brand new industries, but to transform and renew existing sectors. We must make sure we seize that opportunity, building on the world class knowledge and expertise in our universities, colleges and research establishments.

4.4 The convergence between communications and computing will transform business processes and offer new opportunities for innovative products and services. Achieving a rapid and comprehensive roll-out of the next generation of communications infrastructure in the next few years will be key to our efforts to improve the competitiveness of all businesses. Spread of best practice and understanding of emerging new ways of working online will also be vital.

4.5 This chapter shows the key actions Government will take to encourage investment in R&D and infrastructure so that business can exploit new technologies and markets. These include:

- promoting the commercial exploitation of research, focusing on genomics, basic technologies and e-science;
- encouraging development and take-up of more resource efficient and environmentally friendly products and energy systems, and promoting markets for new technologies which reduce waste;
- encouraging diffusion of new technologies such as broadband across homes and businesses;
- boosting digital TV, which will transform the communications services available in the home and open up new markets and service opportunities;
- stimulating the development of content for the digital technologies; and
- increasing awareness and understanding among all businesses of the challenges and opportunities of e-business, and new ways of working in transformed organisations.

Our Goal

4.6 Our goal is to strengthen the ability of British business to innovate. We must do more to promote the exploitation by business of scientific advances in the key technologies of the next decade. We must ensure that all have the skills and capabilities to do so. The benefits must be available to small firms as well as medium and large companies, and in all parts of the country.

Where the UK Stands

4.7 Since 1997, the Government has strengthened our capabilities in science and technology, committing an extra £1.7 billion with the Wellcome Foundation to maintain our world class science base. The White Paper *Excellence and Opportunity: a science and innovation policy for the 21st Century* (Cm 4814 July 2000) set out a full analysis of the UK's position and an agenda for action by Government, academia and business.

4.8 With only one per cent of the world's population, the UK is responsible for 4.5 per cent of the world's spend on science, produces eight per cent of the world's scientific papers and nine per cent of citations. Yet British business fails to make the most of this resource – for instance, our companies apply for fewer US and EU patents than any of our main competitors except Italy. It is not enough to generate excellent research. We must do better at translating scientific advances into new industries, new jobs, and a better quality of life for all our people.

4.9 We must also embrace the green industrial revolution. Businesses increasingly need to develop environmental products and processes in order to meet national and international environmental targets, to meet consumer demand and to improve their competitive position. As part of this, we need to ensure that the UK is at the forefront of renewable energy technology. Photovoltaics – generating electricity from daylight – is a renewable energy source with enormous potential. Yet at present we lag behind Germany, the USA and Japan in developing photovoltaic energy and the supply industries that support it.

Investing in new sources of business success

4.10 New communications infrastructure is needed to enable everyone to benefit from the opportunities of the modern economy, while minimising the potentially undesirable environmental impacts of such development. Our international competitors are racing to roll it out, particularly broadband communications networks and digital TV. In the UK more than one in four homes has been connected to digital TV in the last two years, and we have a universally recognised, highly creative digital content industry. But one third of British businesses with an Internet connection (weighted by employment) simply use the public telephone network system, with no additional digital technology, to increase data transmission speeds. There are risks that we will fall behind the leading nations, and that not everyone will benefit from broadband, particularly outside the more prosperous metropolitan areas.

4.11 In 1998 the Government recognised the importance of encouraging small businesses to get connected to the Internet, setting a target to increase the numbers with a website or making frequent use of external e-mail or electronic data interchange from 350,000 to 1.5 million by 2002. In the event, we had already reached 1.7 million by summer 2000, and now over 90 per cent of businesses (weighted by employment) have an Internet connection. The value of business to business sales in the UK conducted over the Internet is greater as a proportion of output than in any of our leading competitors except the USA. However, the engagement of many businesses in electronic commerce is still relatively shallow: very few businesses are going beyond e-commerce to adopt new ways of working. A further step change is now needed if British business is to stay ahead and capture the full benefits of doing business over networks.

Exploiting the Power of Science

4.12 In addition to the £1.7 billion new investment in science and engineering, we have created a range of partnerships to bring together business and academic researchers and help universities and colleges build their capacity to work with business. We have enacted a string of tax measures to promote enterprise and R&D, particularly benefiting small firms, including manufacturers. We are now examining the case for further measures to encourage R&D among large as well as small companies.

4.13 The Government has already set out its research priorities for the next three years – genomics, e-science and basic technology. We believe these offer the most outstanding opportunities for industrial application and economic growth. We must also look ahead and identify the key areas for future investment in research. The Quinquennial Review of the Research Councils, which will fully involve industry, has been asked to consider how this might be done.

Foresight

The Foresight programme supports the production of independent reports which anticipate the changes which may affect the industrial landscape. The programme has a role to play both in increasing commercial exploitation of new technology, and in ensuring spending on R&D is well focused to meet future needs and market opportunities.

Businesses are supported in accessing this thinking, and in developing their own visions of the future, through close collaboration between the Small Business Service, Regional Development Agencies and the Foresight programme.

For instance, the Manufacturing 2020 Foresight Panel concluded that manufacturing is redefining itself as a provider of lifetime service around a manufactured product, and that the Internet is a major enabler which will initiate a paradigm shift in manufacturing. As a consequence, they recommended that companies should increase their focus on high added value products and technologies, while strengthening their supporting service offerings and actively seeking strategic alliances.

4.14 We must ensure that we maximise the return the nation gets from our investment in research. We must create the conditions in which it reaches and renews existing industries and generates new ones. That means making sure universities and other research establishments have the capability and the incentives they need to reach out to the wider world of business and the community. In particular, we will consider the recommendations from the Council of Science and Technology's current review of the linkages between science and technology and the 'new economy'.

4.15 In some areas our research-based industries are already strong, and we are working with industry to build on these. For instance, a high level Government and industry Pharmaceuticals Industry Competitiveness Task Force has been examining ways to strengthen the UK business environment for this successful research-intensive industry in order to make it still more competitive, and will report to the Prime Minister in the Spring.

Bradford Particle Design plc

BPD plc was established in 1994. The company was formed by Bradford University staff and exploits original university work on particle formation using supercritical fluids.

Supercritical fluid technology has been researched for some years, but the degree of control achieved by the BPD process has expanded its effectiveness and applicability enormously. The BPD process has been evaluated by the pharmaceutical industry, and is destined to be widely applied for the manufacture of a broad range of particulate medicines. BPD developed the technology with the assistance of DTI Smart R&D grants, and DTI-supported LINK grants.

Strong links are maintained with Bradford University. The university is significant shareholder in BPD and is represented on the company's board. The company uses university technical resources and the two organisations collaborate on a number of research projects.

BPD's pioneering research and development has resulted in their acquisition by US drug development company Inhale Therapeutic Systems – a significant development that will strengthen commercial opportunities and growth potential for this Bradford based business.

Investing in new sources of business success

Harnessing Genomics

4.16 Biotechnology is expected to have as revolutionary an impact in the twenty-first century as the computer has had in the twentieth. The mapping of the human genome, completed in July 2000, is one of the most significant scientific achievements in history. Huge opportunities will arise from gene sequencing in the next decade.

4.17 Other countries are making concerted efforts to overtake the UK's lead in biotechnology in Europe. Our aim is to maintain our lead and ensure the UK reaps full economic advantage from our leading position in the biosciences.

4.18 The Government has increased funding for genomics research by an additional £110 million. Our bioscience industry must be properly equipped to make a commercial success of researchers' achievements.

The Government will bring forward a new £25 million programme Harnessing Genomics. This will help businesses take up this rapidly developing science and apply it in new ranges of commercial products, processes and services which will give us health care improvements and environmental applications of real social and economic value.

4.19 The programme will show how science can be harnessed – not only for new medicines and new ways to treat diseases such as Parkinson's, Alzheimer's and cancer – but also using DNA and proteins in novel applications in fields such as electronics and bio-computing. It will provide the tools to support bio-medical developments, particularly bio-informatics which is essential to make use of the very complex data from genomics. In addition, the programme will encourage bio-manufacturing, which is a high priority area for a new Faraday Partnership.

4.20 To give young biotechnology companies a boost, we will help them learn from experienced business gurus in the USA (which has the most developed biotechnology industry) and encourage e-mentoring. We will also encourage provision of the incubator space and advice these companies will need as they develop their growth strategies.

Basic Technologies

4.21 The Government is setting up an interdisciplinary Research Council programme on basic technology worth £41 million over three years. It will support research into the creation of fundamental new capabilities in areas such as quantum computing, sensors, photonics and nanotechnology, which have the potential to transform whole manufacturing sectors and to form the basis of major new, resource efficient industries of the future.

We need to ensure that this research is fully exploited by industry. We will therefore invest £25 million over three years in a series of new activities and projects to ensure that businesses can commercialise such key technologies. The programme will focus on exploiting technologies with widespread applications in manufacturing.

4.22 We are already taking steps to support mature industries in taking advantage of new opportunities. Technical textiles is a global growth market, covering a diverse range of applications from construction materials and conveyor belts through to airbags and high tech composites. British companies have already established world leadership in some of these areas, such as non-wovens. The Government is funding the establishment of a Faraday Partnership for technical textiles, which will strengthen the research base for the sector and enable it to develop stronger links to manufacturing companies. In addition, it will continue to support a range of individual projects aimed at developing new technical textile materials and applications.

E-science

4.23 The next generation of the world wide web will be developed in the coming decade, and like the Internet will create enormous new opportunities for business and commerce. Systems are now being developed which will allow thousands of times more data to move extremely quickly around whole networks. Information will come with tools to allow users to analyse, probe, and process it.

4.24 We must ensure that the UK can lead the way in developing this next generation of information and communications technologies (ICT). It will allow companies to be truly global in their thinking, with whole projects being worked on simultaneously at several sites and all details available to all partners in real time. It may even lead to a new generation of e-commerce, providing customers with a fully interactive service. We are already investing £98 million in research into e-science.

4.25 With these funds we will establish a substantial generic research programme funded jointly by Government and industry to investigate and exploit the underlying network and software technologies of the next generation Internet.

We will complement this with a new £20 million programme over three years to ensure the findings of this research are quickly taken up and turned into commercial applications in the UK. A further £20 million over four years will go towards the establishment of a new Interdisciplinary Research Centre.

4.26 This will bring together manufacturers and researchers to work on interoperability and the commercial applications of new e-technologies.

Vocean

Vocean is a small company in Omagh that worked with the Faculty of Informatics at the University of Ulster, using the TCS scheme (previously known as the Teaching Company Scheme), on developing emerging Internet technologies. As a result, the company now claims to be the market leader in e-procurement products. Graduate Declan Gribbin was the TCS Associate for the Programme that also led to the formation of a new spinout company, 8over8, in which the University has a stakeholding. This new company is now valued at over £25 million and the TCS Associate and academic supervisors are shareholders and directors in the joint venture company located at the University's Science Research Park in Londonderry. Vocean's unique position in the market has resulted in partnership deals with the key industry players and it has grown from a micro-business to one employing over 30 with plans to grow by a further 100 per cent in 2001.

Green Technology and Energy

4.27 The global market for environmental goods and services is currently estimated at $335 billion – comparable with the world markets for pharmaceuticals or aerospace – and is forecast to grow to $640 billion by 2010. In order to exploit this growing demand, the UK needs to be among the front runners in a green industrial revolution.

4.28 In the past, companies have focused primarily on increasing labour productivity. That has been essential in order to overcome the productivity gap with our international competitors. It remains essential because the gap is still too big. Gaining in importance, especially in the future, is environmental – or resource – productivity: maximising our use of renewable resources and minimising waste. This is good for the environment. It also makes good business sense – improving efficiency, cutting production costs, reducing dependency on finite resources.

Investing in new sources of business success

4.29 Business must embrace this challenge by making environmental considerations part of mainstream business activity. Government's role is to provide the support and conditions for new, environmentally sustainable industries to grow, to work with business to improve environmental productivity, and to use government procurement to encourage the take-up of green technologies, while ensuring value for money. The UK has a strong research base in environmental technologies and many leading businesses in some of these industries. Our aim is for the UK to become a leading player in the new markets for green energy and products, waste minimisation, recycling and re-use.

R Griggs and Co Ltd

R.Griggs and Co Ltd is one of the UK's largest footwear manufacturers. It produces the famous Dr Martens brand and employs about 2,000 people. The company hosted trials, which were part-funded by DTI, to evaluate the effectiveness of a biological system to treat volatile organic compound (VOC) emissions. It was so impressed with the results of the trials that it installed a biotrickling filter, which degrades VOCs to water and carbon dioxide.

The new biological system enabled the company to comply with current legislation. A BIO-WISE case study found that the system was 16 per cent cheaper than conventional systems and cost 23 per cent less to run. In addition, it has superior environmental performance compared to conventional incineration.

Howard Johnstone, Group Administration Director said, "We are delighted to have found such a clean and environmentally sound solution to our needs through this use of biotechnology. We are also very proud to be one of the first UK companies to use biotechnology in this sort of application".

Waste

We will commit an additional £10 million to the new Waste and Resources Action Programme to develop new markets for recycled materials and to promote technologies and processes which reduce waste.

4.30 This programme will support investment on a much larger scale in novel methods for waste minimisation, reuse and recycling and to develop new markets. We will also explore the scope for further year on year increases in funding.

4.31 We will launch a Performance and Innovation Unit study of the longer term issues concerned with resource productivity and renewables, and develop specific strategies with the Regional Development Agencies to support the growth of environmental industry clusters across the country.

4.32 The Regional Development Agencies will promote best practice in construction and sustainability, as outlined in the White Paper *Our Towns and Cities: The Future* (Cm 4911, November 2000), to promote innovation and reduce the levels of embodied energy in new housing construction.

Climate Change

4.33 Climate change is a worldwide environmental threat. It has both global and local implications. The devastating floods, droughts and storms we have seen in the UK and across the world in recent years show how vulnerable we are to climate extremes.

4.34 Tackling the causes of climate change will require action across national economies. The actions we propose to take in the UK are described in *Climate Change – the UK Programme* (Cm 4913, November 2000). One of the key elements in this strategic programme is action by business to cut out energy waste across industry and commerce, and to explore and exploit home and export markets for new low carbon technologies.

4.35 We propose to help meet this challenge by setting up joint government business initiatives spearheaded by the 'Carbon Trust'. Announced by the Prime Minister in his speech on the environment in October 2000, this UK wide initiative breaks new ground in the way we approach a major environmental threat. With initial funding of around £50 million per year, the Carbon Trust will:
- work with business to develop a range of information and advice programmes;
- take forward the development of the enhanced capital allowances scheme for approved energy efficiency measures;
- support research, development and demonstration projects; and
- contribute to the development of a long term strategy to move the UK towards a low carbon economy, ready to respond to the climate change challenges and opportunities which lie ahead beyond 2010.

4.36 By supporting renewable energy in the UK, we can also ensure that British industry is well placed to exploit the growing global demand for renewable energy technology.

We will embark on a major initiative with industry and others to achieve a UK solar photovoltaic demonstration programme in line with those of our main competitors.

4.37 Solar photovoltaic (PV) systems, which generate electricity from daylight, are a renewable energy form with enormous potential. Their current contribution to energy supplies is small, but growing rapidly with the aid of substantial support and investment around the world. PV tiles and modules can be incorporated into the roofs of homes and the facades of offices, enabling buildings to generate their own electricity.

4.38 The programme we propose, subject to approval by the European Commission, will establish the UK as a credible player in the PV market, alongside Germany (100,000 roofs by 2007) and Japan (70,000 roofs by 2002). It will encourage R&D and manufacturing investment in this field in the UK. We will also encourage British industry to move direct to the innovative thin-film technologies, which have greater potential for cost-reduction than existing technologies, thus giving them a lead in exploiting overseas markets as well.

4.39 Social housing refurbishments will be one of the key target groups for this programme. We can use PV to help alleviate fuel poverty as well as helping us to achieve security of energy supply and environmental objectives.

4.40 We also need to take advantage of the opportunities offered by market liberalisation, advances in technology and the development of renewable generation. The Government has established an industry wide working group to examine how the commercial and regulatory environment will need to adapt to enable industry to take advantage of these changes.

4.41 The Group published its report on 17 January 2001, recommending a wide range of actions to encourage the development of renewable energy and combined heat and power, by enabling small scale generation to be connected to the local distribution network. The Group has now put its report out to consultation until early March, and will then finalise its recommendations.

Broadband

4.42 Broadband networks will give us the next leap forward in communications capability. Whether provided by cable, fibre, upgraded copper lines, wireless or satellite, they support the services which modern businesses need to stay competitive, including always on access to the Internet, high quality video transmissions and rapid exchange of bulk data. DTI research shows that businesses with an Internet connection using digital technology are 80 per cent more likely to engage in e-commerce than those with just an analogue connection to the public telephone network.

Our goal is for the UK to have the most extensive and competitive broadband market in the G7 by 2005, with significantly increased broadband connections to schools, libraries, further education colleges and universities. As an initial step, we will:

- *set up a new £30 million fund over the next three years to support innovative schemes to meet local requirements, to see how we can ensure that as many people and businesses as possible across the UK have access to affordable broadband services; and*
- *use more effective procurement of the public sector's broadband requirements to improve value for money, encourage the private sector to speed up further roll-out, and in particular to drive broadband into rural areas. We will start with an audit of bandwidth requirements in 100 market towns.*

4.43 We are also publishing *UK Online: the broadband future* (available online at www.e-envoy.gov.uk), a report to the Prime Minister by the e-Minister and e-Envoy, on how we can achieve this aim. The report outlines the steps we will take to ensure a competitive and dynamic market in broadband services, offering value and choice to businesses and consumers in the UK.

4.44 If we are to make the most of communications technology, we must ensure that as many people and businesses as possible across the UK can access affordable broadband services, especially small businesses. We will identify how best to achieve this in every part of the country. A new fund of £30 million over the next three years will support the Regional Development Agencies and devolved administrations in taking forward innovative schemes to meet local requirements for extending broadband networks, building on international best practice. The Countryside Agency will monitor the roll-out of broadband in rural areas, and we will take this into account in developing policy.

4.45 We will promote industry investment in higher bandwidth services so that as many people as possible can receive, and send, complex data services such as video. We will redouble our efforts to ensure that the regulatory environment provides the maximum degree of encouragement for investment in such services. This will include vigorous action to complete the unbundling of BT's local loop and to release more radio spectrum.

4.46 We must keep up our investment in broadband for key parts of the public sector. The Government's objective is world class broadband links for all schools. The DfEE is already investing nearly £80 million from the Standards Fund over 2000-02 to start providing schools systematically with broadband access to the Internet.

4.47 We have commissioned a study from NM Rothschild to consider how we can ensure schools reap the benefits of leading technology in the long term most cost effectively as demands for bandwidth grow. The study will report later this month and we will then take decisions that will ensure that we achieve our objective.

| 4.48 | We will also ensure that we make the most of public investment in broadband. Around £500 million is likely to be invested over the next three years to provide broadband connectivity to schools, colleges, universities, libraries, hospitals, doctors' surgeries, police stations, UK online centres and other public sector locations. We will identify ways of aggregating this public sector demand, particularly with a view to facilitating broadband roll-out in regions where broadband companies may otherwise find it uneconomic to do so. To assist this, the Countryside Agency will fund a 'health check' for 100 market towns to identify their needs. This will include the current and future availability of broadband services, and an audit of the potential public/private sector demand for broadband in each town.

| 4.49 | We also recognise that infrastructure on its own is not enough; we need to address a range of wider issues if the rollout of broadband is to be a success. Content is a key driver of the take-up of digital technologies. We have a thriving digital content industry, made up of Internet publishers, new interactive media and computer games developers and others, and we will continue to support its development. We will work with the industry, primarily through the Digital Content Forum, to ensure that the content sector seizes the opportunities offered by broadband. Pilot programmes will be developed to stimulate the development of local broadband content.

| 4.50 | Development of broadband applications could also be held back if there were a shortage of suitably qualified engineers or of those with the mix of creative and technical skills needed to create broadband content. These issues are addressed in Chapter 2.

| 4.51 | The Government will continue to work closely with industry to identify the critical issues and develop solutions. We will establish a UK online Broadband Stakeholder Group, chaired by the e-Minister, as the focus of this work. We will initiate a major programme of research to inform future policy as the broadband market develops, and be prepared to take further action if this proves necessary.

Digital Television

| 4.52 | We also need to make sure that Britain leads the world in the development of digital television, and that every community shares in its benefits. Digital television will transform the communications services available in the home. Using technology that people understand and are comfortable and confident with, we will be able to provide a learning resource and communications centre in every livingroom. It puts control of viewing in the hands of viewers rather than broadcasters. Choice will increase, and the potential of teletext will be unleashed by use of graphics and high speed updates. Combined with a phone line, it can give everyone access to the Internet in their living rooms, stimulating computer literacy in the population as a whole. It will offer new Internet-based learning opportunities and interactive services, making e-shopping and e-banking more attractive for many people and opening up new opportunities for business products and services.

| 4.53 | Ensuring that we are at the forefront of digital television will help our broadcasting and communications industries improve their competitive position, extend consumer choice through e-commerce and open up new learning opportunities for everyone.

Our aim is for the UK to have the most dynamic and competitive market for digital TV in the G7, as measured by take up, choice and cost. As the first part of our strategy to achieve this, we will:
- *bring together key public and private sector stakeholders to develop a comprehensive digital TV action plan;*
- *work with the broadcasters and others to launch a series of digital TV projects in 2001, giving participating communities the opportunity to help shape the future of digital TV;*
- *work with the broadcasters to promote public understanding of the benefits digital TV can offer; and*
- *work with the industry to ensure clearer and more informative labelling of digital TV services and equipment.*

4.54 Our broadcasters, manufacturers and retailers have put the UK at the forefront of the digital TV revolution. We will capitalise on this through a range of new initiatives. DTI and DCMS will work with key players in the public and private sector to develop a comprehensive action plan to maximise the benefits of digital TV. This will involve broadcasters (such as the BBC and ITV companies, Channel 4, Channel 5, BSkyB, OnDigital, NTL and Telewest), transmission companies (such as Crown Castle), equipment manufacturers (such as Pace and Sony), retailers (such as Dixons) and consumer/viewer groups (such as the Consumers' Association). Discussions with these organisations have indicated a clear interest in working together to develop such a plan and have uncovered a wealth of positive ideas and scope for creating a powerful and effective public/private partnership.

4.55 We will launch several small scale pilot projects offering free conversion to digital TV to defined communities, in partnership with the Independent Television Commision and the industry, to understand better the use that people will make of the new technology, including those who only want free-to-air services. These projects will include access both to free-to-air digital TV channels and to interactive services, including the Internet.

4.56 We will start by offering conversion to a small number of households and build up rapidly to convert a wider community of a thousand or more households. Those taking part in the projects will be given intensive support so that we can establish viewer requirements and assess whether they are being met by the equipment and services under development. As a result, the communities selected will have an opportunity to help shape the future of digital TV.

4.57 In parallel, we will develop a clear labelling scheme, in consultation with the industry, to ensure everyone understands what services are available and what equipment they need. We will also review the potential impact of digital TV on energy use in the home and how we can ensure that equipment is as energy efficient as possible.

4.58 Together with the broadcasters (particularly the BBC, ITV and Channel 4) we will also promote public understanding of the benefits of digital TV. This work will complement the industry's marketing of pay-TV services by focusing on the other benefits of digital TV, such as extra free-to-air channels, interactive services and Internet access.

4.59 The digital infrastructure and e-business will create many opportunities to secure greater resource efficiency and environmental improvements, but we cannot take these potential benefits for granted. The Government, together with an industry consortium, is therefore supporting a project, Digital Futures, to advise on how to secure these gains.

Model of e-adoption ladder
Adapted from Cisco led Information Age Partnership study on e-commerce in small business

Business benefits ↑

- **e-mail**: Efficient internal and external communications
- **website**: Place in worldwide market / Window on worldwide suppliers
- **e-commerce**: Order and pay online, reducing transaction costs / Maximise accessibility and speed
- **e-business**: Integrate supply chain so manufacture and delivery become seamless / Minimise waste at every stage of the supply chain
- **transformed organisations**: Open systems of information for customers, suppliers and partners / New business models based on interworking between organisations and individuals

→ *Extent of organisational change and sophistication*

Enabling e-business

4.60 As well as developing the communications infrastructure needed to compete in the future, we need to ensure that business makes the most of the opportunities it offers. This is not just a matter of connecting to the Internet or having a website, important though that is. It is also about changing the ways in which businesses organise themselves and how they work with customers, suppliers and other partners, as illustrated above.

4.61 It is up to each individual business to adapt the tools of e-commerce and e-business to enhance its efficiency and trading capability. But identifying the opportunities and making the leap are major challenges. This is where Government can help.

Delap and Waller

Delap and Waller is a firm of mechanical and electrical consulting engineers with regional offices in Belfast, London, Derry, Dublin, Cork and Sligo employing 150 staff. It saw the opportunity to share information better between staff in its different offices and with customers in order to streamline its business processes and provide speedier and more efficient services for clients.

It installed a Wide Area Network (WAN), remote access and desktop and video conferencing. These now enable it to form virtual teams from across its offices and wider within its sector when bidding for new work. Integrating the technology throughout the business was responsible in part for a £600,000 (almost 15 per cent) increase in turnover against difficult trading conditions. According to MD Liam O'Hagan, "This will allow us to offer better service to our customers and also liaise more closely with project partners and the supply chain."

Investing in new sources of business success

UK online for business, the Government programme which helps firms get online, will spend an additional £30 million over the next three years to help businesses move beyond having a website or trading online to transform themselves through the effective use of ICT. The Government will also use its procurement programme to encourage businesses to take up e-business technologies.

4.62 The Government is providing a package of support for small businesses to increase their capability to use ICT. As a result, small enterprises wanting to improve their ICT equipment and skills can benefit from the following:

- a dedicated service through UK online for business advisers in every Business Link that will provide impartial, practical, hands-on advice and assistance for small firms to help them use ICT in their business. Under this programme Business Links will develop a range of services tailored to meet the differing needs of individual small firms;
- a range of showcasing, demonstrators and other best practice activities giving practical examples of the business benefits from using ICTs;
- 100 per cent first year capital allowances for investment in computers, software and Internet-enabled mobile telephones over the next three years;
- guidance and support services tailored to the needs of individual sectors and regions.

4.63 DTI is also working with members of the Information Age Partnership, involving the UK's leading suppliers of ICT equipment and services, and with other UK online for business partners to highlight the benefits of information age technologies. This will include an E-Business Improvement Week, offering:
- free initial advice from Partnership members;
- seminars and workshops; and
- industry open days.

4.64 The Government has provided an additional £30 million for UK online for business to extend these activities. This will enable UK online for business to work with industry and others to help put British business into the lead in the emerging new ways of working online, moving beyond just having a website or trading online to transforming business practices.

4.65 The Government will also use its procurement programme to encourage businesses to take up e-business technologies and practices. All tendering for government contracts will be conducted online by 2002. The Office for Government Commerce, Department of Trade & Industry, Small Business Service and key purchasing departments will work together to develop learning opportunities and advice for smaller businesses, to enable them to use Internet technologies to participate in a wide range of procurement activity. As purchasers, these departments will also promote the use of e-tendering in ways which will actively encourage smaller businesses to bid for contracts electronically.

4.66 We will also open up opportunities for the private sector to develop products using Internet technology to simplify business dealings with Government, such as payroll and tax or VAT returns. To achieve this we will open up access to the 'back offices' of government departments to those potential providers, where appropriate using the new Government gateway to ensure security and privacy. We will continue our drive to modernise the delivery of other public services, as we have with NHS Direct.

4.67 As a result, we want UK industry to be a world leader in key sectors through the take-up of e-business practices and new online ways of working. We want more extensive use of e-business in all sectors to help close the productivity gap between the UK and our main competitors.

4.68 We must also create an environment which nurtures new and emerging Internet based businesses. The Government is therefore launching a £5 million Internet mentoring initiative to help Internet start-ups and established small and medium sized firms who want to make the Internet their primary means of doing business. Under the initiative, companies will be able to access tailored business advice via a new interactive web portal. The initiative also includes an Internet incubator fund which will stimulate the creation of new regional incubators specifically to support and nurture new e-businesses, particularly in areas where they currently have less support.

4.69 We also need to do more to give consumers the confidence to make use of these new technologies. Growth in this form of commerce is currently being held back by a lack of confidence in the integrity of online markets. We will help the private sector to develop the TrustUK scheme, which approves good e-commerce codes of conduct. Internationally, we will develop better collaboration between enforcement agencies in different countries, especially in those countries where British consumers are most likely to shop over the Internet.

4.70 We have already established arrangements – amongst the first of their kind – with the US Federal Trade Commission on co-operation against Internet crime. This year we will sign agreements with Canada and Australia. We will also launch a UK Dispute Resolution Clearing House – as part of a Europe wide scheme giving consumers access to alternative dispute resolution schemes across the European Union.

Consumers Driving Innovation and Competitiveness

4.71 Knowledgeable and demanding consumers are a positive force in promoting competitiveness. As markets become global, consumers are becoming more sophisticated and more demanding: demanding value for money, expecting quality and design, searching wider markets.

4.72 To ensure that consumers have the knowledge they need to act as a spur to innovation and quality we are raising the profile and quality of consumer education and advice. We will set up Consumer Support Networks throughout the UK, which will provide quality assured, better co-ordinated and more accessible advice services for consumers.

Investing in new sources of business success

A WHITE PAPER ON ENTERPRISE, SKILLS AND INNOVATION

5 A climate for enterprise and growth

Introduction

5.1 Entrepreneurship has become a critical part of the social, political and economic agenda around the world. Britain needs a business climate which supports the rapid creation of many more new and innovative enterprises, so vital to the dynamism of our economy. Our business climate must help – and never hinder – the growth and success of all of our companies, new and old. In the fierce global fight for capital, skills and investment, our business climate must help us attract the best people and overseas firms to the UK.

5.2 Government's role is to create the business, financial and regulatory framework needed to realise this vision and to remove unnecessary barriers to enterprise. Government must help create an ambitious business culture, which enables people from all walks of life to realise their creativity, innovative ability and entrepreneurial potential. We must help any person with the will and the ability to create and grow a successful business. And honest business failure should not mean that you cannot ever have another go.

5.3 We have already done much to promote a more entrepreneurial climate in the UK. This chapter shows the additional key actions we propose to take, including:
- significantly relaxing insolvency rules so that honest businesses and individuals who go bankrupt have a better chance of starting again quicker, while cracking down on the fraudulent and irresponsible; and
- a new pro-competitive role for the Office of Fair Trading to spot existing and proposed regulations which hold back dynamic and competitive markets.

Our Goal

5.4 Our goal is for the UK to be recognised as the enterprise hub of Europe. Our business climate, regulatory framework and social attitudes towards business success – and failure – must be attuned to meeting this goal.

Where the UK Stands

5.5 Since 1997 we have taken action across a wide range of areas to encourage a more favourable entrepreneurial climate:

- against upheaval and uncertainty in global markets, a key task has been to create predictability in the economic environment through low interest rates, low inflation and consistent policies on tax and regulation. With the lowest rates of corporation tax ever in the UK and a stable macroeconomic environment, businesses can focus on the competitive challenge;
- competition and anti-trust laws have been updated. We have announced a new approach to mergers which is more transparent and imposes the least possible burden on the business community, whilst promoting consumers' interests. We have strengthened consumer protection policy; our new Consumer Enforcement Forum brings business, consumers and enforcers together to help achieve more coherent consumer protection. We have implemented an Electronic Communications Act which will transform the way Government works and interacts with its citizens and businesses. We have produced a *Communications White Paper* (Cm 5010) which sets out a new framework for communications regulation;
- we have made clear our commitment to a major overhaul of company law. We expect an independent review team to produce wide-ranging and detailed proposals for consideration in May, with a clear 'think small first' approach;
- through our Fairness at Work agenda – with measures such as the National Minimum Wage, the Employment Relations Act 1999 and the Working Time Regulations – we have put in place a framework designed to promote fairness in the workplace and support the development of a modern, flexible labour market;
- we will continue to ensure that the labour market framework promotes competitiveness, assessing regulatory proposals against the four criteria that they should encourage labour market participation, encourage the acquisition and retention of skills, promote flexibility and mobility, and support the development of good relations at work;
- we have promoted investment in new technology from the UK High Technology Fund, launched in July 2000, which has now reached its target investment level of £125 million. The fund is investing through specialist fund providers including Merlin Bioscience, Amadeus, Advent and MTI. It is helping to support a range of technologies including novel vaccines; ultra-cheap plastic microchips to endow everyday products with 'intelligence'; a new cardiac monitoring method; new cancer therapies and a new WAP search engine. The fund will also support a new method of electronic protection for intellectual property transmitted across the Internet.

Fender Sturrock Ltd

Whilst studying for a law degree Jenine Parkynn did numerous part-time promotions for the drinks industry. This gave her the idea for her own thriving company, Fender Sturrock, which she set up November 1998. The promotions and marketing company provides blue chip clients with skilled staff for publicity campaigns at clubs, pubs and trade shows across the UK. They also provide marketing ideas for product launches and promotions and carry out field marketing activities for major banking institutes. Starting out of a tiny office in Edinburgh, Fender Sturrock now employs 225 full-time staff across the UK.

Urban Splash

Tom Bloxham MBE and Jonathan Falkingham have founded no fewer than five companies, collectively called Urban Splash. Their business, with a turnover of £14 million, is based on property development. Tom and Jonathan were the first people to create loft living spaces outside London and their work is highly rated by regeneration agencies, such as English Partnerships. They have a reputation for taking on sites that other property companies will not touch and turning them into desirable locations. Their inspiration comes from the oath of the ancient Athenians – loosely translated as 'leave our city not less, but greater, better and more beautiful than it was left to us'.

5.6 The UK compares well to its competitors in terms of its business and regulatory framework. The Institute of Management Development Survey 2000 found that we have the second most supportive institutional and political environment among the seven leading industrial nations. OECD data suggest that in the UK the corporate tax burden is relatively light compared with the rest of the EU. The business environment we have created is both pro-competitive and pro-innovation. Many aspects of our labour market are highly flexible, compared to other countries. But in a fast moving global environment, where other nations are not standing still, we must continue to work hard to maintain and improve on this relative advantage.

5.7 The UK also compares relatively well on the conditions for entrepreneurship, particularly in the commercial and professional infrastructure and the developed venture capital industry. But according to the Global Entrepreneurship Monitor (GEM) Report 2000, we also lag our competitors in significant respects. In particular, the level of new business start-ups is significantly behind countries like the USA, Australia and Canada, and the entrepreneurial culture – particularly the tendency to identify and exploit business opportunities – is not well developed.

The Inner Tube

Inspired by the way recycled tyre inner tubes are used to make products ranging from water carriers to shoes in many third world countries, Julie McDonagh began to test market the commercial opportunities in the UK for products made from recycled inner tubes. She identified a market for high fashion bags and hand luggage, and started her business in 1996 with a £2,000 loan from The Prince's Youth Business Trust and £1,000, which she raised by selling her car. Initially, Julie operated from a small factory unit using a second hand sewing machine to produce 10 bags a week for a handful of customers.

Four years later the business has grown from producing ten bags a week to 200 per day. Her products, which also include bikinis, vases, sunglasses cases, cosmetic bags and mirrors, are now sold in 50 designer stores in the UK, and are exported as far afield as New York and Hong Kong with distributors worldwide. Over the last year exporting has become a major part of the business, and currently accounts for 60 per cent of turnover.

January 2001 saw the opening of the first Inner Tube retail outlet in Portsmouth. Inner Tube Ltd has also secured contracts with large buying groups who require exclusive designs. In 1999 Inner Tube launched its website www.innertube.co.uk and has seen a steady growth of sales in this area.

What the Government will do

Enhancing Entrepreneurial Culture and Modernising Insolvency Law

5.8 We need to promote the acceptance across our whole society that identifying opportunities and exploiting them with a new business is appropriate as a career choice and can make a contribution to the good of society as a whole. The Global Entrepreneurship Monitor Report 2000 identified this as one of the key issues to address in increasing further levels of entrepreneurial activity in the UK, together with that of education on business skills.

5.9 Entrepreneurship involves balancing potential risks with possible reward. For many business people, success comes only after numerous attempts. We should not deal with business failure in a way which creates a barrier to future success.

5.10 An entrepreneurial economy needs to support responsible risk taking. Insolvency Law must be updated so that it strikes the right balance. It must deal proportionately with financial failure, whilst assuring creditors that it is handled efficiently and effectively. The law currently makes no distinction between someone whose bankruptcy comes about as a result of their fraud, and someone who fails because they have, for example, guaranteed a company's bank overdraft.

To encourage more business people to start or re-start businesses after failure, we will radically reform Insolvency Law. We will ensure that those whose failure is honest are not punished or stigmatised, while at the same time increasing the penalties for those who set out to defraud, and those who are otherwise culpable.

5.11 For individuals in England and Wales, we will sweep away many of the outdated and unnecessary restrictions which apply to all bankrupts, regardless of their culpability, as we already have for London taxi drivers – such as being a member of Parliament, a school governor, a trustee of a charity, or a local councillor. We will also cut by two thirds, to 12 months, the maximum default period during which people against whom a bankruptcy order has been made are subject to the remaining restrictions, with the majority being discharged much earlier. But we will do more to identify those whose failure is irresponsible, negligent, or dishonest, and make them subject to restrictions for up to 15 years.

5.12 In addition, we will investigate the viability of providing a single scheme, unifying bankruptcy and the County Court Administration procedure, to deal with all personal insolvency.

5.13 For companies we will introduce new legislation, as soon as Parliamentary time allows, which will bring business insolvency law and practice right up to date. We are consulting on possible further measures to help promote a rescue culture. These will build on the changes already introduced in the new Insolvency Act 2000, which will make it easier for companies in difficulty, particularly small firms, to reach voluntary arrangements with creditors and speed up the disqualification of unfit company directors.

5.14 Last November we announced the adoption of a more commercial approach on the part of the Inland Revenue and Customs and Excise to rescue proposals put to them by companies in short term financial difficulty. We also announced that a new Inland Revenue/Customs and Excise Unit will be set up from 1 April 2001 to ensure that:
- rescue proposals receive individual consideration and are considered in the same way as commercial creditors; and
- the Inland Revenue and Customs and Excise publish and stick to strict timetables in dealing with proposals.

5.15 The Revenue departments will also ensure that their staff have a better understanding of the problems businesses face. Businesses and ultimately all taxpayers will see real benefits from this more commercial approach.

Competition and Markets

5.16 Strong competition in our domestic markets makes for strong businesses. It provides a spur for firms to innovate, increase productivity and provide real choice for consumers. It equips them to compete in the global market place. Conversely, anti-competitive behaviour is a burden on the economy; a burden on businesses which want to grow by offering better value; and a burden on ordinary consumers who have to pay more for less. Cartels and abuse of market power stifle the growth of new businesses. As technologies and business strategies change, so too do the dynamics of monopoly and competition.

5.17 Regulation is vital to the effective functioning of markets, and to achieving our social and environmental objectives. It can, however, have unintended impacts on the dynamics of markets. We need to ensure we fully achieve our legitimate regulatory objectives without imposing undue burdens or distorting competition.

To encourage more businesses to start up and compete in new markets, we will give the Office of Fair Trading (OFT) and other regulators a new role to assess when laws and regulations create barriers to entry and competition, or channel markets in a particular direction, thereby holding back innovation and progress.

5.18 The OFT will:
- with assistance from DTI and other Whitehall departments, identify key sectors where competition concerns have been identified and undertake in-depth studies to examine the need for action. Ministers are currently considering a report the OFT has submitted on restrictions on competition in certain professions. In some sectors there may for instance be unnecessary barriers to new entrants based on outdated analysis, or regulatory requirements. These may focus excessively on inputs, perhaps requiring expensive investment (for example the need for a particular type of machinery) rather than on outputs (for example meeting a particular safety or quality threshold);
- draw the Government's attention to any regulatory barriers to entry which emerge during investigations under competition powers; and
- work with the Regulatory Impact Unit and other Whitehall Departments in order to provide Ministers with more information about the impact of proposed regulations on competition.

5.19 It would be open to the devolved administrations to make similar use of the OFT's expertise if they so wish.

5.20 It will remain the responsibility of Ministers to weigh up the many important factors affecting any individual regulatory decision.

5.21 We will also keep under review the new competition regime introduced through the Competition Act 1998, to ensure it is working effectively to encourage dynamic competition and prevent companies with market power abusing their position in any way. If the new regime proves to be too weak, we will consider sensible improvements drawing on international experience. Greater co-operation between competition authorities is part of this process. We will work with the USA and the EU on exchange of information in anti-trust cases.

Regulation and 'Think Small First'

Regulations are not an end in themselves – they should enable markets to operate effectively, fairly and safely. Regulations are not intrinsically anti-business. They benefit businesses by opening up markets and enabling newcomers to compete on equal terms with existing companies. They spur innovation by imposing new standards of quality and safety, for example in the environmental field. By increasing consumer protection, for example in e-commerce, they widen market potential and demand for more products.

Rights at work…

The knowledge economy is changing working patterns. The UK's regulatory framework must keep up with the evolving workplace. The Government's role is to facilitate adaptation to these new conditions on fair terms. Rights at work are not the same as red tape. Minimum regulatory standards encourage partnership in the workplace, promote social inclusion, and give employees confidence. Employers also benefit. Reputable firms are protected from unfair competition. Workers are more motivated if allowed to balance their work and private lives. Staff turnover and absenteeism are reduced.

Avoiding over-regulation…

But we recognise the risks of over-regulation and the disproportionate effect it can have on smaller firms. It is the Government's role to support small businesses to meet the challenges of the twenty-first century. That is why the Government published 'Think Small First' in January 2001. It asks every government department to think about their role in supporting small business and developing an entrepreneurial society. The Government has asked the Small Business Service (SBS) to drive forward Think Small First and asked all departments to consult the SBS at an early stage whenever UK regulations are being considered. Working with other departments, the SBS will aim to reduce the burden of compliance for existing regulations and will consult small business to ensure their voice is heard at the heart of Government. We are already acting on these aims, for example, the Prime Minister recently announced new arrangements to give businesses more time and guidance before new laws are introduced. The Small Business Service will launch the Business Link National Information and Advice Service in April 2001. This will provide a single point of access to advice and guidance on a wide range of regulatory and business issues.

The Best Financial Climate for New Business and Growth

5.22 We have already looked in Chapter Three at the availability of finance to business. It is also crucial that we provide the right financial environment to encourage the flow of finance from individuals, companies and institutions to business.

5.23 An essential prerequisite for the development of the venture capital market and other forms of early stage finance is an available 'exit route' through a trade sale or initial public offering (IPO). The environment for IPOs for fast growing technology companies has improved with changes to the Listing Rules now enabling technology companies to obtain a listing without needing a three year trading record.

Further initiatives are planned. The Financial Services Authority will shortly be launching a full-scale review of the UK Listing Rules to look at updating and, where appropriate, streamlining requirements. However, given the central importance of this area to growth and competitiveness, the Government will continue to keep under review the effectiveness of quoted equity markets as exit routes available to venture capitalists.

5.24 We have also asked Paul Myners to conduct an independent review of possible distortions to institutional investment decision-making that discourage investment in small and medium sized firms. He will report in time for this year's Budget.

5.25 We will further improve the fiscal environment through proposals announced in the Pre-Budget Report to reduce the impact of VAT on small businesses. We will also expand the Enterprise Management Incentive Scheme to help smaller companies recruit more key employees, and we have introduced measures to reduce the uncertainties arising from National Insurance liabilities created by share options.

5.26 Besides ensuring that firms have access to the finance they need at all levels, it is equally important for firms to know what external investment is on offer and what it means for them to take the plunge. Some firms may hold back from seeking external finance because they are unsure about the practicalities and worried about the complications. Others may not be aware that they are in a position where external finance can help them out or can facilitate a new level or dimension of operation.

The Small Business Service (SBS) will therefore launch, by the summer, a set of initiatives to help small businesses understand external investment better and become better prepared to take it on. We will be looking for innovative approaches to assist small firms on this issue and will encourage interested parties to come forward with a range of ideas on how the SBS can support, build on and spread best practice, using the Business Link network as appropriate.

Intellectual Property

5.27 More businesses are recognising that competitive advantage comes from knowledge and new ideas. That means companies must develop and protect intellectual property. It is therefore hardly surprising that there has been an explosion in patenting, particularly in the USA. We need to ensure that British businesses have every opportunity to benefit from the system internationally. Innovation and ideas must be adequately rewarded at home, particularly through patent protection.

Intellectual Property Boosts the Bioscience Sector in Manchester

ManIP is a very successful Manchester based consortium, supported by the DTI's Biotechnology Exploitation Platform Challenge, which aims to help the transfer of intellectual property into industry. The UK is very strong in bioscience but the UK public sector is poorly equipped to manage its intellectual property to benefit UK companies. Several universities, NHS Trusts and technology transfer organisations are collaborating to turn science into products. Launched in 1998, the consortium has identified 120 good ideas which are ripe for exploitation, and has some 35 patents.

5.28 To encourage more UK firms to file and get patent protection more effectively, the Government is committed to reform of the European and international regimes by:

- continuing to push for EU patent protection that is as simple and inexpensive to obtain as its international equivalents, via agreement on a single Community Patent by the end of 2001. This will allow British and other European businesses to protect their entire home market via a single patent, as their US counterparts can in the USA;
- pressing for measures to reduce the time and cost of taking out and defending patents, for example via further reform of the European Patent Organisation and a quicker and more uniform litigation process. To promote increased international co-operation we will seek to align the European Patent Convention more closely with other international agreements; and
- pressing for better protection of digital content on the Internet through the construction of an international copyright framework.

5.29 As a further encouragement to British firms, the Patent Office will look at how they can make the patent system more helpful for small firms. We will also work with Universities UK and the Association of University Research and Industry Links to ensure that universities also improve their management of intellectual property in line with leading private, public and international practice. A recent development has been the launch of an Intellectual Property Web Portal, which acts as a gateway to a wide range of advice on IP rights, and results from work initiated by the Creative Industries Task Force.

Delivering Support for Business

5.30 Many businesses find Government business support confusing and difficult to access. We need to deliver help more quickly and with less bureaucracy, taking full advantage of advances in technology. And we need to identify more effectively the forms of support that best meet business needs.

5.31 We will market our support in a way which responds more directly to business needs. The Small Business Service will establish the Business Link National Information and Advice Service as our key channel for informing firms about the support available. We will also reduce the bureaucracy under each support scheme, and set a goal for processing applications for DTI and SBS support schemes within 30 days, depending on their complexity.

5.32 We must ensure that DTI works effectively across Government to create the right conditions for the growth industries of the future. To achieve this, we will set up cross-functional teams with a broad membership drawn from Government and the private sector. These teams will identify and tackle barriers to growth and target practical and measurable improvements in performance against international competitors.

Improving Services through Electronic Government

Interactions with Companies House will be transformed. Over the next decade paper forms and microfiches will gradually become a thing of the past. Companies will be able to update their own records and access information through powerful search tools.

The Insolvency Service will have full electronic capability. Multi-channel access will be provided for customers, many of whom are 'technologically excluded' by becoming bankrupt. The Service will build on e-business networks with the Small Business Service, the courts, the Stationery Office and the Inland Revenue, so that all its routine dealings will be electronic.

The Patent Office will have all its key services available online by 2005. Renewals, searches and filing of applications for patents, trade marks and designs will all be available at the click of a mouse.

The Small Business Service will launch the Business Link National Information and Advice Service in April 2001. This will provide a single point of access to advice and guidance on a wide range of regulatory and business issues and will be supported by a call centre giving direct access to a network of locally delivered, high quality business advice services. It will also provide tailored advice to women starting up in business for the first time, as well as established women entrepreneurs.

Regional Selective Assistance and Enterprise Grant applicants can access the DTI's and Government Office's websites for guidance and application forms. A full online service should be available by 2002. We are streamlining RSA procedures to fit better with companies' own planning, and to devolve more decisions to the regions.

A WHITE PAPER ON ENTERPRISE, SKILLS AND INNOVATION

6 Global ambition

Introduction

6.1 In the last two years economic interdependence among nations has grown closer – especially between the countries of Europe. Capital and people are even more mobile. New technology and ideas are spreading ever faster across borders. Goods are made wherever the conditions are best, marketed electronically and then transported worldwide. The international trade in services is growing.

6.2 These changes will bring huge benefits to consumers, businesses and their employees in the UK, Europe and the rest of the world. They can also bring threats. Employees find their existing skills are no longer in demand. Businesses see their traditional markets threatened or taken away, as they struggle to compete with cheaper imports at home or new competition overseas. Many communities and regions are finding that the industries on which they built their economic success in the last century are no longer a secure basis for prosperity in the future.

6.3 The previous chapters of this White Paper show how the Government is helping to sustain this prosperity by supporting individuals, businesses and communities in the UK as they respond to new challenges. We must create in the UK a climate for enterprise and growth which provides the best platform for business to compete in Europe and worldwide. But if we are to secure prosperity at home, we must also be active abroad in helping to create the conditions for British business to succeed. This chapter sets out the additional measures the Government will take in pursuit of this aim.

6.4 We must move forward by engaging actively and constructively in Europe and the wider world to promote British interests. We must continue to work at the international level to open up markets and drive forward economic reform in Europe and across the world. By building links between people, partnerships between businesses, and harnessing the potential of all our regions to compete worldwide, we can strengthen our global connections and help build economic success at home.

Pentwyn Splicers

Two years ago, Pentwyn Splicers was under severe pressure. This small Pontypool firm which manufactures splicers – machine tools used in the textile industry for joining yarns cleanly, without knots – was watching its business disappear with the migration of textile manufacture overseas. It became vital for the company to make good a decline in UK turnover by increasing the export sales of two highly competitive new splicers (subsequently Millennium Product Award winners). Lessons learned from a project on e-business, run by Cardiff University, were incorporated into customer support activities. Managing Director Graham Waters used information technology as a cost effective means of informing potential customers, around the world, of Pentwyn Splicers' new competitive products. Significant new business was secured in Poland, South Korea, Saudi Arabia, Turkey and Japan. As a result, exports now represent 70 per cent of total sales. Pentwyn Splicers continue to operate in an extremely competitive market but Graham Waters is optimistic about the future, 'We are seeing the stirring of sales in markets where we've never been before'.

6.5 In pushing forward these changes, national governments must also be realistic about the limits of their power. In a global economy we benefit from investment by multinational companies which can go anywhere in the world. We cannot force companies to invest or re-invest in particular places. But we expect their decisions to be responsible ones. Government can help to lead people through change and it can help influence the wider international framework within which the decisions of businesses and individuals are made. We must also ensure that we harness the benefits for poorer countries. The Government's recent White Paper *Eliminating World Poverty: Making Globalisation Work for the Poor* (Cm 5006) set out our strategy for achieving this.

6.6 This chapter shows how the Government will work to strengthen the UK's global links, and promote the best environment for British success in Europe and worldwide. To do this it is critical that we win the global battle for talent. Therefore we will:

- establish a new Enterprise Scholarship scheme for the brightest and best young graduates – particularly in high tech subjects – who want to come to the UK to develop their careers and start new businesses. We will also pilot a scheme to encourage British entrepreneurs abroad to establish companies in the UK to pursue innovative business ideas;
- strengthen our support for British business on the global stage by launching a global partnership programme to help our firms into international collaboration at home and overseas, with the world's best as their partners;
- work to improve the framework for closer global economic integration and ensure that it contributes to sustainable development for all, by preparing for a new round of comprehensive World Trade Organisation negotiations; and
- promote a better business environment in Europe by setting in hand, in consultation with our European partners, a major study of the benefits to our people and businesses of achieving European economic reform. Just as the Cecchini report in the 1980s was a powerful reminder of the need to press ahead to reap the economic benefits of the single market, so we will use this study to maintain pressure for progress towards the Lisbon goals.

Pan Global Solutions (PGS)

PGS is an IT recruitment specialist and solutions provider that draws on a worldwide database of 25,000 consultants in e-commerce, programming and specialist IT fields to provide bespoke teams that deliver the complete team solution to client needs. PGS's primary product is people; people with the knowledge, skills and experience to meet client needs. The fact that PGS does not restrict its offering by location has helped it to achieve a rapidly growing database of clients and consultants. Clients include British American Tobacco, Cadbury Schweppes, Nokia, Sun Microsystems and Saudi Aramco amongst many others.

In the short term PGS have plans for a New York office. Longer term, there are plans for offices and consulting centres in South Africa, San Francisco, India and Australia.

www.panglobal.co.uk

6.17 We must help British business respond to these challenges by ensuring that support for businesses operating in global markets is second to none. We will invest £20 million over the next three years to transform the online operations of Invest UK and Trade Partners UK to meet the changing needs of business.

We will launch a new global partnership programme to help businesses build links with international partners, at home and abroad.

6.18 The programme will strengthen partnerships at home and overseas. Complementing the new approach to regional policy set out in Chapter 3, its key focus will be in the regions, with the objective of building global partnerships across the UK. Invest UK and Trade Partners UK will work with regional business and academic networks to strengthen existing links, matching regional business strengths to international markets. This will be taken forward with the Development Agencies in England, Scotland, Wales and Northern Ireland.

6.19 To help more businesses exploit the advances in science and technology worldwide, we will also promote partnerships with leading overseas sources of technology, focusing on the areas identified by the Foresight Programme as critical to UK competitiveness. As well as strengthening the science and technology expertise available at key embassies abroad and doubling the number of International Technology Promoters who help British businesses access new technologies and develop partnerships in technology with their leading counterparts overseas, we will pilot a new inward secondments programme to bring overseas technology experts to work with British companies. We will also provide businesses with enhanced information on technology developments and opportunities overseas, through our online service *globalwatchonline.com*.

Tyne Slipway

Tyne Slipway and Engineering Company, a small family owned business, is to branch out into boatbuilding and foresees the creation of twenty jobs in two years.

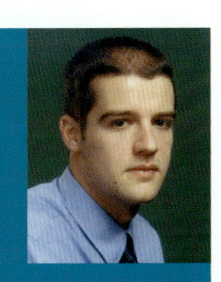

Harry Wilson, managing director, sees the move as part of his vision to bring commercial boatbuilding back to the Tyne through the introduction of the concept of selling boats in 'flat packs'.

The knowledge gained from a DTI supported secondment to the Netherlands studying state-of-the-art computer modelling software will be used with traditional Tyneside shipbuilding skills as part of his vision. Harry Wilson is already in discussions with an American boat builder regarding possible sales. The company previously used the secondment service to study ship repair techniques in Norway. This was part of a process which resulted in them being appointed exclusive UK and Eire sales and service agents for a Norwegian company producing ship propulsion thrusters. They subsequently increased their staff from four to ten.

6.20 Inward investment to the UK plays a key role in helping to strengthen international links. As part of the partnership programme, we will devote new resources to strengthen investment in the UK from existing and emerging high technology markets. We will also help to stimulate partnerships and links between foreign partners and the UK's best firms and centres of excellence, and encourage existing investors to expand their operations in the UK through an enhanced aftercare service.

6.21 We will also help companies that have previously only traded in the UK to develop the skills and ambition to build international links, by rolling out a national programme to help new exporters. Its emphasis will be on training and skills for the new international business environment, including e-business. Services for new exporters will also be simplified in a single package.

Arima Optoelectronics Limited and the University of Bath

Taiwanese owned Arima Optoelectronics (UK) Ltd has invested £850,000 in a semiconductor growth system in a new laboratory facility in the Physics Department of the University of Bath. This facility is the first of its kind in the UK, and Arima contributes £300,000 per year to sponsor the research chair of Professor W N Wang and four other researchers to develop cost effective approaches to manufacture power efficient blue light emitting diodes (LEDs). The blue LEDs developed in Bath produce brightness compatible with the most efficient in the world and have the potential for a range of commercial applications.

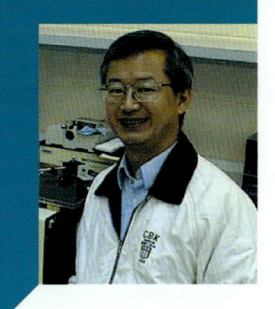

Improving the Framework for Closer Global Integration

6.22 The integration of global markets means more opportunities for the UK, but we need agreed standards, clear rules and fair dispute mechanisms. This means working with others, including in Europe, the G8 and the Commonwealth, to improve the governance of the global economy. We must strengthen and reform global economic institutions such as the World Trade Organisation (WTO), the International Monetary Fund (IMF), the World Bank and United Nations (UN), so that they can better respond to the challenges ahead, and help ensure that globalisation brings benefits for developing countries as well as richer nations. We must also develop our co-operation in new areas such as the Internet and biotechnology.

6.23 The WTO plays an important role in helping to establish the conditions in which businesses can strengthen their international links through trade. The case for continuing to push forward its development through a new round of comprehensive negotiations is clear. Halving barriers and improving procedures to facilitate trade in goods and services could boost world incomes by £270 billion per annum. In today's terms, that is equivalent to over £40 for every person on earth. To help us realise these potential benefits we need to work towards the removal of unnecessary barriers, and to seek to ensure that new barriers are not erected. We also have the opportunity to make a major contribution to sustainable economic development for all nations.

6.24 The UK must exploit its international links – within the EU and the Commonwealth, and with other influential countries – to help start the new round of negotiations. We need to help build confidence in the WTO amongst all members, by providing practical assistance and ensuring that developing countries play a full part in its decision-making processes. We need to improve dispute settlement procedures, for example the way WTO decisions on disputes are implemented. And we must work with other countries to consider ways to reform the WTO itself and ensure greater openness in the way it operates.

6.25 Comprehensive negotiations under the WTO also have the potential to help deliver wider benefits. We want the new round to deal not only with improving access to markets but also with the relationship between trade rules and environmental polices, and with rule-making on issues such as international investment and competition.

Reform in Europe

6.26 The EU is the UK's home market. Over three million jobs depend on trade in goods and services with EU countries worth over £300 million every day. Promoting the development of the single market and the creation within the EU of a dynamic, entrepreneurial economy are vital for sustaining British competitiveness. Economic reform in Europe will enable the UK, like all EU Member States, to take advantage of the changes in the global economy we are now seeing. We also need to ensure that within the UK, both nationally and regionally, European funds are used effectively to promote enterprise and growth.

6.27 We want to work closely with business to identify the most important remaining barriers to completion of the single market and the most effective solutions in removing them. The Chancellor of the Exchequer and the Secretary of State for Trade and Industry will be holding a series of seminars with business leaders during February, covering key areas such as manufacturing, services, telecoms and utilities, to help shape the Government's approach in the run up to the Stockholm summit in March 2001 and beyond.

6.28 The meeting of the leaders of EU Member States in Lisbon in March 2000 set the agenda for making Europe the most dynamic and knowledge based economy in the world by 2010. Its conclusions created a strategy for ten years of economic reform to achieve this goal. They represent a step-change in economic policy for the EU. The rewards are high – but so is the price of failure. We must continue to build momentum, and will work with all EU Member States to ensure delivery of the strategy for economic reform agreed at Lisbon. The first review of progress against the Lisbon objectives will take place at the Stockholm summit.

6.29 The programme of economic reform in Europe agreed at Lisbon has the potential to bring higher growth, greater productivity, and more jobs.

We will be setting in hand, in consultation with our EU partners, a major study to quantify the benefits of economic reform in Europe and make clear what the rewards are for continuing reform and the costs of failing to push forward. Just as the Cecchini report in the 1980s was a powerful reminder of the need to press ahead to reap the economic benefits of the single market, so we will use this study to maintain pressure for progress towards the Lisbon goals.

6.30 We will also work with our partners to drive forward the process of improving the climate for innovation by benchmarking Europe's position against its competitors through a major study on biotechnology.

6.31 The UK now receives substantial funding from the EU. The Government will promote best use of this funding to ensure that it is invested in projects which bring long term benefits to our people and our economy.

A Strategy for European Economic Reform

Communications For electronic commerce and the Internet to flourish we must complete the liberalisation of telecommunications markets by the end of 2001, combined with swift EU action to promote e-commerce and ensure a pre-competitive regulatory framework.

Research & Development at both national and EU level must be refocused towards the technologies of the future. We will be pressing for such a reprioritisation in the forthcoming negotiations on the new European Framework Programme. We must reward innovation and new ideas adequately, particularly through fast and efficient patent protection.

Regulation We are pushing forward the modernisation of Europe's approach to regulation so that the needs of small businesses are put first, through robust impact assessments, greater consultation, and examining alternatives to regulation. We also support the pilot project by the Commission looking at the impact of new regulations at the EU level. The Stockholm Council will need to give a further push to this programme for better European regulation.

Finance for Growing Businesses It is important that the EU establishes guidelines to allow rapid approval of national venture capital schemes to respond to the needs of growing businesses. We also need to see innovative use of European Investment Bank finance in order to redirect funding towards support for business start-ups, high tech firms and micro-enterprises, as well as other risk capital initiatives proposed by the Bank.

Single Market Liberalisation European leaders agreed in Lisbon to speed up liberalisation across a range of services such as energy and financial services. We want to see this accelerated through decisions this March at the Stockholm summit.

Education and employment We must promote opportunities for all European citizens to develop their skills, especially in information and communications technology (ICT), and the entrepreneurial skills needed to create a more dynamic enterprise culture. The Government will work towards agreement at Stockholm on new measures to enhance lifelong learning and foster ICT skills, involving business.

European Funds

European structural funds support measures for regional economic development, employment and training, and for improving agriculture and fisheries. As a result of the Government's success in negotiations at the 1999 Berlin European Council, the UK is due to receive some £10.7 billion from European structural funds for 2000–06. Over £7 billion will go to programmes run by local partnerships in disadvantaged regions.

To date, much of the support from structural funds has contributed to infrastructure and regeneration in regions suffering from industrial decline. For example, the Lowry project in Salford received over £15 million from the **European Regional Development Fund**, which allowed the development of new public facilities such as theatres and art galleries. Transport infrastructure has also received European funding, such as Manchester's Metrolink and Inverness airport. The emphasis is now shifting towards enterprise, innovation and small businesses. For example, the Coventry TechnoCentre received a grant of over £5 million to develop premises for new business start-ups and development, technology transfer and training. **The European Social Fund** helps with training both for unemployed people and those in work. For example, a project at Bridgend College in Wales received £125,000 to provide training in electronics and engineering with the aim of promoting innovation in small businesses.

The **European Investment Bank** (EIB) provides finance to aid regional development and to help the achievement of other EU objectives. The EIB is owned by the 15 EU Member States and raises its funds on the capital markets. In the past it has typically lent for large construction projects in transport, telecommunications, energy and industry. At the Lisbon European Council, the UK successfully pressed for the EIB to expand into funding knowledge based industries, innovation and education. The EIB will lend up to £9 billion across the EU over the next three years to support these new areas. In recent years, EIB lending in the UK has averaged £1.8 billion per year. The EIB, together with its risk/venture capital arm, the **European Investment Fund**, also provides venture capital for high technology small and medium sized enterprises. The EIB was a launch investor in the UK High Technology Fund. Chapter 3 describes several new EIB initiatives in the UK which are underway or under consideration.

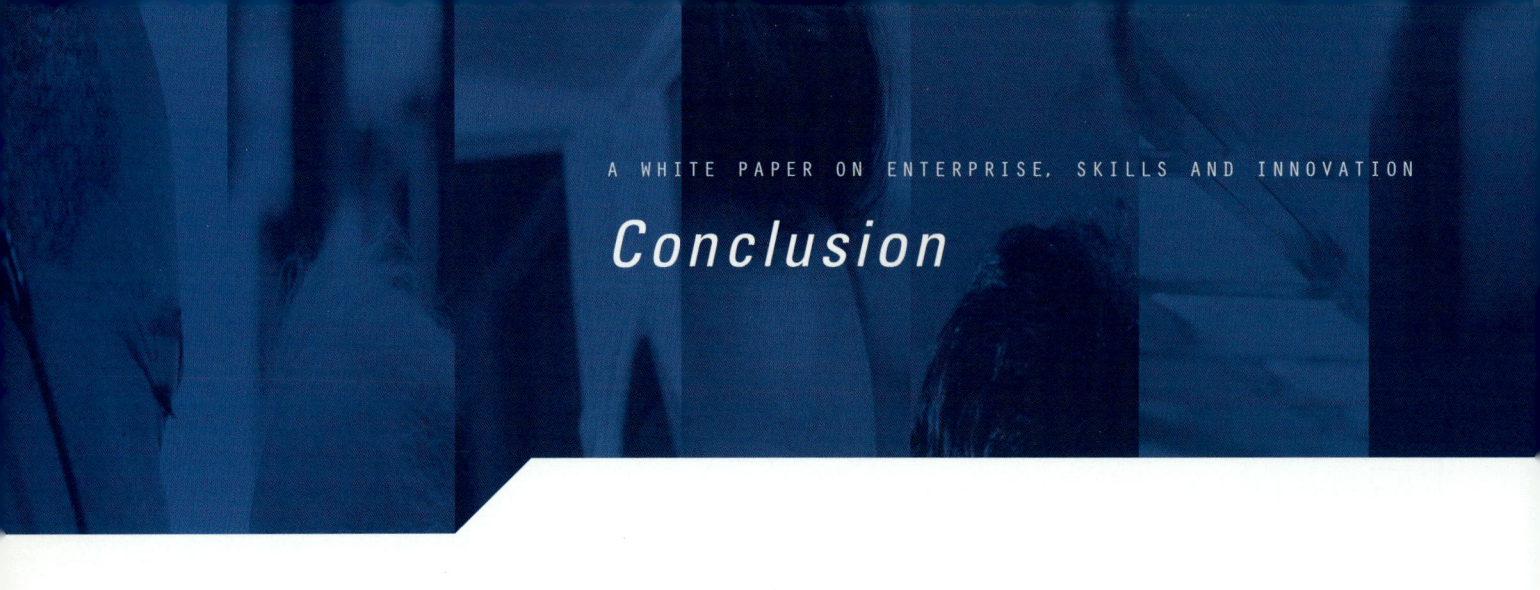

A WHITE PAPER ON ENTERPRISE, SKILLS AND INNOVATION

Conclusion

The Government is committed to creating the conditions for individuals, business, communities and regions to succeed in this fast changing world. This White Paper, on which the Department of Trade and Industry and Department for Education and Employment have worked closely together, draws powerful links between the skills of individuals, the enterprise of communities and regions, innovation in business and the research base and our ability to move forward as a nation.

We have strengthened substantially the ability of the UK to respond to the challenges of globalisation, technological advances and rising skills needs but there is no room for complacency. This is why we have focused on a set of initiatives and actions in five key areas: developing a more highly skilled workforce; building strong regions and communities; spreading the benefits of new research and technologies and developing new world-beating industries; ensuring markets operate effectively and fairly; strengthening our position in European and global trade.

We will shortly be publishing an implementation plan to show how we plan to put the key initiatives into practice. This is Government's side of the bargain. But the recipe for success lies in the efforts, creativity and entrepreneurial spirit of individuals in businesses, communities and regions. This White Paper sets out the framework which we believe will bring success over the next decade. But delivery of success lies in the hands of people to whom it is addressed.

If you have any comments on the White Paper,
you can send them to :

The Rt Hon Stephen Byers
Secretary of State for Trade and Industry
1 Victoria Street
London
SW1H 0ET
e-mail address: opportunity.forall@dti.gsi.gov.uk

or

The Rt Hon David Blunkett
Secretary of State for Educations and Employment
Sanctuary Buildings
Great Smith Street
London
SW1P 3BT
e-mail address: opportunity.forall@dfee.gov.uk

The text of the white paper is also available on
www.dti.gov.uk/opportunityforall or through the DTI
and DFEE homepages at
www.dti.gov.uk
www.dfee.gov.uk